17 September 2010

Rose*

Wi

Postwar Japanese Economy

Mitsuhiko Iyoda

Postwar Japanese Economy

Lessons of Economic Growth
and the Bubble Economy

 Springer

Mitsuhiko Iyoda
St. Andrew's University
  (Momoyama Gakuin University)
1-1 Manabino
Izumi-shi, Osaka 594-1198
Japan
m-iyoda@andrew.ac.jp

ISBN 978-1-4419-6331-4   e-ISBN 978-1-4419-6332-1
DOI 10.1007/978-1-4419-6332-1
Springer New York Dordrecht Heidelberg London

Library of Congress Control Number: 2010928699

Printed on acid-free paper

Springer is part of Springer Science+Business Media (www.springer.com)

Preface

Will economics prevent the crises occurring throughout the domestic and world economies? Looking back at the development of economic science, we have never been able to reduce the intrinsic instability of economic societies. However, we can analyze the fundamental cause of crises and suggest countermeasures for relaxing or solving the cause. It will be impossible in most cases to prevent the negative aspects of capitalism. We have not always prepared effectively for the downside of every economic problem, particularly new types of serious economic phenomena. Unexpected problems have appeared one after another. In addition, there are wars and tyranny, which destroy economic performance in the world.

We trust in the development of economic science to remedy the maladies and to solve serious economic problems and contribute to enhancing the satisfaction level of humankind. Viewing some lessons from the Japanese experience in this connection, we have learned the following:

First, the result of rapid economic growth itself did not always mean the growth of economic welfare. This was caused by the limitation of *GNP* (applied to *GDP*) concept, leading to the development of *NNW* concept and Happiness Research. In these four decades, there has been much literature regarding this question. This is an example of the development of economic science to examine the human need on a higher level.

Second, as a result of the bubble economy and its consequences, people experienced catastrophic burdens. Human wisdom could not avoid this phenomenon. Economic science could not forecast it, but we will become clever by learning from the bubble experience. We hope economics will help us to find some ingenuity to relax or weaken the causes of economic instability.

Finally, in the concluding chapter, I propose a basic design toward achieving a high satisfaction level society, that is, the quality of life in the mature society which we should seek.

I hope this book will interest specialists, students, and any reader who wishes to understand economic science and the Japanese experience in this context.

This book is based on my lectures entitled, "Introduction to the Japanese Economy" (spring) and "Bright and Gloomy Sides of the Postwar Japanese Economy" (fall) at Momoyama Gakuin (St. Andrew's) University. These lectures are conducted entirely in English as semester courses, particularly for overseas exchange students, as well as Japanese students. The lecture has started from the 2004 fall semester. The lecture in the spring semester is for the undergraduates and that in fall semester for both the undergraduates and the postgraduates. I have tried to make the lecture more comprehensive by using charts and tables as much as possible. However, I should like to leave it up to the reader's judgment as to whether or not my attempt is successful.

Osaka, Japan   Mitsuhiko Iyoda

Acknowledgments

I hope that this book will partially redeem the many debts, both intellectual and personal, that I owe to others.

I am thankful to Martin Ricketts (professor at Buckingham University) and Michael Ward (former chairman of International Association for Research in Income and Wealth, IARIW). Professor Ricketts kindly gave me the opportunity to speak at an international studies seminar at the University of Buckingham in 2006 and 2008. I spoke on "Bright and Gloomy Sides of the Postwar Japanese Economy" and "The Bubble Economy and Its Consequences: The Japanese Experience." I received a good response from the participants, which gave me great stimulus to write a book. Mr. Ward suggested that I present a paper at IARIW–NBS (National Bureau of Statistics, China) international conference held in 2007. The paper was entitled, "Postwar Japanese Economy: Some Cautionary Lessons for China from the Japanese Experience," which attracted strong interest from the participants. I am also thankful to the seminar and the conference participants, and my lecture students.

I owe much to my former supervisors, Professors Kent Mathews at Cardiff Business School and Jim Rafferty at Buckingham University, who offered many suggestions about my seminar topics. Furthermore, I am grateful to the large body of literature, particularly the works of Nakamura (1995), Tsuru (1993), Ito (1992), and Itoh (2000), all of which inspired me to write this book. It is with sadness that I acknowledge the passing of Michael in October 2008. He showed a keen interest in my seminars, and he greatly encouraged my writing, but regrettably, I did not finish my first manuscript until the end of 2008. I vividly remember us taking a walk and discussing the book on a beautiful day in Cambridge.

After that, I received a favorable and constructive review of the manuscript from the publisher, suggesting some points for improvement. During the summer of 2009, I was engaged in this improvement at Buckingham University. I wish to thank those reviewer(s). Suffice to say that the responsibility is my own for any misleading points and remaining errors in this book. I also wish to thank Jon Gurstelle, Economics and Policy Editor at Springer, for his kind consideration in the process of publishing this book

Finally, I would like to thank both St. Andrew's (Momoyama Gakuin) and Buckingham Universities for giving me the opportunity to do my research. For many years, especially during the summer, Buckingham University, has provided me precious opportunities to develop my research and my relationships with many academics. My family patiently allowed me to live a separate life, and I should like to offer a special thanks to Masako.

Osaka, Japan   Mitsuhiko Iyoda
January 2010

Contents

Abbreviations

ASEAN	Association of Southeast Asian Nations
BIS	Bank for International Settlements
BoJ	Bank of Japan
CAO	Cabinet Office
CD	Certificate of Deposit
CMEPSP	Commission on the Measurement of Economic Performance and Social Progress
Cominform	Communist Information Bureau
CPI	Consumer Price Index
CV	Coefficient of Variance
DPJ	Democratic Party of Japan
DCPI	Domestic Corporate Price Index
DNA	Department of National Accounts
Emp. C	Employee's Compensation
EPA	Economic Planning Agency
ESA	Financial Service Agency
ESRI	Economic and Social Research Institute
FIES	Family Income and Expenditure Survey
FIL	Fiscal Investment and Loans (*Zaisei Toyushi*)
FIL-GNE ratio	(Financial Investment and Loans)/(Gross National Expenditure) Ratio
FSS	Family Savings Survey
FY	Fiscal Year
GATT	General Agreement on Tariffs and Trade
GB	Government Bond
GDFCF	Gross Domestic Fixed Capital Formation
GDP	Gross Domestic Product
GFCF	Gross Fixed Capital Formation
GHQ	General Head Quarter
GIOMS	Government Information Office of Minister's Secretariat
GNI	Gross National Income
GNE	Gross National Expenditure
GNP	Gross National Product

GPI	Genuine Progress Indicator
GoJ	Government of Japan
HCLC	Holding Company Liquidation Commission
IARIW	International Association for Research in Income and Wealth
IB	Investigation Bureau
ILO	International Labor Organization
IMF	International Monetary Fund
ISEW	Index of Sustainable Economic Growth
JFEO	Japan Federation of Economic Organization
LDP	Liberal Democratic Party
MCA	Management and Coordination Agency
MEW	Measure of Economic Welfare
MoF	Ministry of Finance
MHLW	Ministry of Health, Labor and Welfare
MIAC	Ministry of International Affairs and Communications
MITI	Ministry of International Trade and Industry
NAFTA	North American Free Trade Agreement
NEET	Not in Education, Employment or Training
NI	National Income
NNP	Net National Product
NNW	Net National Welfare
NPL	Nonperforming Loan
ODA	Official Development Assistance
OECD	Organization for Economic Corporation and Development
PPP	Purchasing Power Parity
PRI	Policy Research Institute
QLPB	Quality-of-Life Policy Bureau
RSD	Research and Statistics Department
SB	Statistics Bureau
SDP	Social Democratic Party
SII	Structural Impediments Initiative
SNA	System of National Accounts
TOPIX	Tokyo Stock Price Index
WPI	Wholesale Price Index
WTO	World Trade Organization

List of Figures

List of Tables

Chapter 1
Introduction

1.1 General View of the Subject

This book is an introduction to the postwar Japanese economy. Some 64 years have passed since the end of World War II. During this period, the Japanese economy has seen rapid changes and remarkable progress, although it has also experienced the bubble economy and prolonged stagnation. What kind of changes have we had in those years? In what sense can we say that progress has been made? What lessons have we learned from the experiences?

The primary aim of this book is to answer these questions. We begin with an overview of the postwar Japanese economy, which is shown by data as historical changes. Then we deal with four major economic issues in the postwar Japanese economy: economic restoration, rapid economic growth, the bubble economy, and current topics. However, our particular focus is on the meaning of economic growth and the bubble economy, and thus this book is entitled *Postwar Japanese Economy: Lessons of Economic Growth and the Bubble Economy*.

Relative to this issue, we must first note that economic growth does not always mean the improvement of our standard of living. This is demonstrated by showing various results of economic growth (both bright and gloomy sides). We explore the category of Gross Domestic Product (*GDP*),[1] demonstrating that the measurement of *GDP* includes market failures theoretically and empirically (factually). This is important because economic growth is generally expressed in terms of the *GDP* growth rate.

Second, to cope with this categorical weakness, a welfare measurement was established. We deal with the measurement and its topic development. The pioneering work on this was a "Measure of Economic Welfare" (*MEW*, Nordhaus and Tobin 1971). Subsequently, a similar sort of measurement called the Net National Welfare (*NNW*, *NNW* Development Committee, Economic Council 1973) was developed. We investigate its properties in later chapters. Further improvement along these lines is the Genuine Progress Indicator (*GPI*). Further developments were broader approaches, which appeared to deal with the human satisfaction level as a whole: that is, social indicators and the measurement of happiness. These approaches are not confined to economic activities but include sociocultural activities trying to capture the total living satisfaction.

M. Iyoda, *Postwar Japanese Economy*, DOI 10.1007/978-1-4419-6332-1_1,
© Springer Science+Business Media, LLC 2010

We have learned that the Japanese economy on the whole has been paying a tremendous cost due to the bubble economy and its consequences including (1) non-performing loans in Japanese banks, (2) huge outstanding government bonds, and (3) prolonged stagnation (so-called 10 year lost age). The Plaza Accord (1985) had a critical effect on the creation of the Japanese bubble, the underlying factor mainly being a huge trade imbalance within each and between Japan and the US. Global capitalism has intrinsic instability and we do not yet know how to cope properly with this problem. In order to avoid future catastrophe and to further stabilize the economy, we may need much ingenuity to offset the damaging effects of market imperfection under the current information society.

Finally, I propose a basic design toward achieving a high satisfaction level society in the concluding chapter. That is the quality of life in the *mature society* which we should seek. This may be one of the important options in the future. The design is based on the discussions in the previous chapters, particularly, lessons of economic growth and the bubble economy.

The basic idea for this book dates back to 1986 when I was asked to give an open lecture to the public entitled, "Postwar Japanese Economy: Bright and Gloomy Sides of Economic Growth." Since then, I have given similar lectures in English to overseas students. From the 2004 fall semester on, I had the opportunity to give this lecture at Momoyama Gakuin (St. Andrew's) University as a semester course for both undergraduates and postgraduates. The lecture, which is conducted entirely in English for overseas exchange students and Japanese students, demands a wider topic coverage. Therefore, I have made an effort to provide compact and comprehensive explanations, using figures and tables as much as possible.

I was invited to speak at an international studies seminar at the University of Buckingham in the summers of 2006 and 2008 by Professor Martin Ricketts. At the first seminar in 2006, I presented part of my lecture given earlier at our university in Japan, which fortunately got a good response. This gave me great stimulus to write a book on this theme. I also presented a paper at an International Conference jointly organized by IARIW (International Association for Research in Income and Wealth) and NBS (National Bureau of Statistics, China), which was held in Beijing in September 2007. The paper was entitled "Postwar Japanese Economy: Some Cautionary Lessons for China from the Japanese Experience," and in the latter seminar, I spoke on "The Bubble Economy and Its Consequences: The Japanese Experience," both of which aroused the strong interest of the participants. I would like to wait for the reader's judgment as to whether or not my attempt is successful.

The following sections are sketches of the Japanese economy. The corresponding chapter explains those in detail with data and references.

1.2 Overview of Postwar Japan

1.2.1 Political Landscape

Table 1.1 shows a brief postwar timeline of Japan and overseas events. Japan surrendered to the Allied Forces in August 1945. From 1945 to 1952 Japan was occupied

Table 1.1 Brief postwar timeline of Japanese and overseas events

Year	Business cycle	Domestic economy	Politics, and others	Overseas events
1945			(8)[a] Japan surrendered; GHQ (set up)	(10) United Nations (founded)
1946		Three major reforms imposed by the GHQ (1946–1950)[b] (12) Keisha Seisan Hoshiki [Priority production system] (introduced)		
1947			(5) New Constitution of Japan (effected)	(3) IMF starts
1948			(10) Second Yoshida administration	(11) GATT starts
1949		(3) Dodge Plan (4) Exchange rate (fixed at $1 = 360 yen) (9) Tax reform (Shoup recommendation)		(8) NATO (North Atlantic Treaty Organization, founded)
1950			(8) Police Reserve Force (set up at MacArthur's direction)	(6) *Korean War*
1951	(6) peak			
1952	(10) trough	(8) IMF (member)	(4) San Francisco Peace Treaty; US–Japan security treaty (effected) (7) National Security Force (formed)	
1953			(7) Self-defense Forces (established)	
1954	(1) peak			
	(11) trough			
1955		(9) GATT (member) (12) First 5-year government plan	(10) Social Democratic Party (reunified); (11) Liberal Democratic Party (formed) (LDP holds power until 1993) (11) United Nations (member)	
1956				
1957	(6) peak			(1) EEC starts
1958	(6) trough			
1959				
1960		(12) National Income Doubling Plan	(6) US–Japan Security Treaty (amended) (7) Ikeda Administration	
1961	(12) peak			
1962	(10) trough			(9) OECD starts

Table 1.1 (continued)

Year	Business cycle	Domestic economy	Politics, and others	Overseas events
1963				
1964	(10) peak	(4) Article VIII Party of the IMF; OECD (member), (10) Tokyo Olympics		
1965	(10) trough			
1966				
1967		(7) Basic Law for Environmental Pollution Control		(7) EC (European Community, founded)
1968				
1969		(6) Second largest GDP nation (announced)		
1970	(7) peak	(3) Osaka Exposition		
1971	(12) trough	(7) Environment Agency (launched) (12) Revaluation of the Yen ($1 = 308 yen)	(6) Okinawa Reversion Agreement	(8) Nixon shock
1972			(7) Tanaka administration	
1973	(11) peak	(2) Floating exchange rate system (Yen) (10) *First oil crisis*		(10) Fourth Middle East War
1974				
1975	(3) trough			
1976				
1977	(1) peak (10) trough			(11) First Summit held in France
1978				
1979		(2) Second oil crisis		
1980	(2) peak			
1981				
1982				
1983	(2) trough			
1984				
1985	(6) peak			(9) Plaza Accord
1986	(11) trough			
1987				(10) Black Monday

Table 1.1 (continued)

Year	Business cycle	Domestic economy	Politics, and others	Overseas events
1988				
1989		(4) Consumption tax (introduced, 3%)		(11) Fall of the Berlin Wall
1990				
1991	(2) peak	*Bubble economy burst*		(1) Gulf War (11) Soviet Union (resolved)
1992				
1993	(10) trough		(6) Split of the LDP (reorganization of political parties) (8) Hosokawa administration (first non-LDP government since 1955)	(4) 8% BIS regulation (11) EU (European Union, established)
1994				
1995			(1) Great Kobe Earthquake	(1) WTO starts
1996			(9) DPJ (founded)	
1997	(5) peak	(4) Consumption tax rate (rose to 5%)		
1998				
1999	(1) trough			(1) Euro (adopted)
2000	(10) peak			
2001	(1) trough		(4) Koizumi administration	(9) 11 September terrorist attacks
2002	(1) trough			(3) US-led war on Iraq
2003				
2004				
2005				
2006				
2007	(1) peak			(8) Financial Crisis (triggered by subprime problems)
2008				
2009			(9) DPJ government	

[a]Month is in parentheses. [b]Antitrust measures: Zaibatsu Dissolution (1946), Antimonopoly Law (1947), and Elimination of Excessive Concentration of Economic Power Law (1947). Land Reform (1946–1950). Labor Reform: Labor Union Law (1946), Labor Relations Adjustment Law (1946), and Labor Standards Law (1947)

Sources: Iwanami Shoten (ed.) (2001). Watanabe, Skrzypczak and Snowdon (eds.) (2003), Chronological Table of Japanese History and Chronological Table of World History. ESRI of CAO (b) (2001–2004), Appendix: Postwar Economic Timeline

by the Allied Forces under General Douglas MacArthur, the Supreme Commander for the Allied Powers (*SCAP*). MacArthur's primary objectives for Japan were demilitarization and democratization. Demilitarization was achieved through the following: the suspension of military production, a ban on fleet and aircraft facilities, restrictions on heavy industries and merchant vessels, and establishment of a new constitution.

Economic democratization consisted mainly of three reforms that were imposed by the General Head Quarter (*GHQ*): Antitrust measures (1946–1947) (Zaibatsu dissolution, and so on), land reform (1946–1950), and labor reform (1946–1947). Other policies that underwent democratization were the education system and the political system, including the establishment of a new constitution of Japan. Guided by the *GHQ*, Japan established a new Constitution of Japan (1947) instead of the prewar Imperial Constitution. Military forces were permanently banned by Article 9 of the constitution. Various forms of democracy were introduced such as voting rights to all adults aged 20 years and older, and the election introduced the House of Councillors (Upper House) as well as the House of Representatives (Lower House). Using the American model for its education system, Japan introduced a 6-3-3-4 system, and coeducation was introduced at the compulsory stage.

Reflecting the deepening of the Cold War, the *GHQ*'s policy changed from that of weakening the Japanese economy to making it a strong ally. For example, the *GHQ* issued a political order depriving government employees of the right to strike (August 1948) and acquiesced in political firings, the "red purge" in 1949. However, important reforms and changes of political and education systems strongly transformed Japan to a democratic society. The power elite was replaced by the young generation.

The San Francisco Peace Treaty restored Japan's sovereignty on April 28, 1952. The occupation of Japan by the Allied Powers ended. The US–Japan Security Treaty (Japanese–American Security Pact) also concluded in 1952. From this date Japan became truly independent as it was able to determine economic policies by itself but continued to rely on the United States for national security.

In 1955, the *LDP* (Liberal Democratic Party) was formed by the merger of two major conservative parties, and the *SDP* (Social Democratic Party) was unified in the same year. The *LDP* held power until 1993 with the *SDP* as the main opposition. This was the so-called "Parties system since 1955." The *LDP's* policy was to protect the capitalistic economic system. The Japanese bureaucrats (particularly central government careers centered on Kasumigaseki, Tokyo) had the real power in policy decisions through legislation. They supported the conservative party, and their ideology was economy-oriented—the quest for Japan to become a great economic power.

A serious political dispute erupted among both political parties and the general public about an amendment of the US–Japan Security Treaty (1960). As a whole, however, political stability was maintained under this system under which the Japanese society and economy developed.

The *LDP*, after the general election (1993), precipitated reorganization of the political party. The Hosokawa administration was launched, which was the first non-*LDP* government since 1955. *LDP* returned to administration in the coalition government as a major party in 1994. Since then, except for a long-lasting Koizumi administration (5 years and 5 months), Japan has almost lost its political stability. (See also Table 8.1 in Chapter 8.)

1.2.2 Economic Landscape

In the following discussion, we roughly classify, by the average growth rate, the Japanese postwar economy into four periods: recovery period (1946–1950), rapid growth period (1950–1973, 9.3 percent), moderate growth period (including the bubble age) (1976–1991, 4.3 percent), and stagnation period (1992–2003, 1 percent) (annual average growth rate in parentheses).

This rough classification is confirmed in Fig. 1.1. We observe an event or a shock between the periods that made a great change in the growth rate. The Korean War (June 1950) took place between the recovery and the rapid growth periods. The special export demand created by this war became the springboard for the beginning of strong growth. The world economy was hit by the first oil crisis (October 1973), which terminated Japan's rapid growth period. Since the collapse of the bubble in the early 1990s, the Japanese economy has stagnated. We examine an economic landscape by period in the next section.

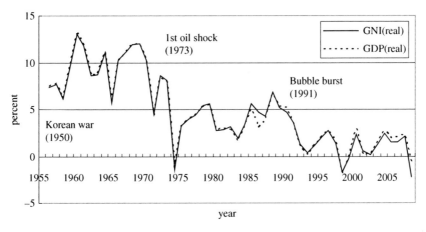

Fig. 1.1 Economic growth.
Source: CAO of GoJ (2009), Long–term economic statistics obtained from homepage (www5.cao. go.jp/keizai/index-e.html#aes). (Compiled by the author)

1.3 Economic Landscape by Period

1.3.1 Recovery Period

As we mentioned above in the political landscape, the *GHQ* imposed three reforms. First were three antitrust measures: dissolution of the Zaibatsu (1946–1951), the enactment of the Anti-Monopoly Law (1947), and the Elimination of Excessive Concentration of Economic Power Law (1947). Second was the land reform, by which the cultivated percentage of farmland by tenant farmers greatly declined to 10 (1950) from 46 (1946). The reform created a middle class because agricultural production increased rapidly. This contributed to income equality and political stability in the agricultural sector in Japan. Third was the labor reform, introducing the Labor Union Law (1946), the Labor Relations Adjustment Law (1946), and the Labor Standards Law (1947). As a result, labor unions spread quickly and the unionized percentage of workers jumped from 3.2 (1945) to 41.5 (1946), then 53 (1948). This increased the number of strikes and labor-management conflicts.

Tax reform was not imposed by the *GHQ*, which was implemented during the occupation period in accordance with the recommendations of the Shoup Mission led by American economist Carol Shoup in 1949 and 1950. A comprehensive income tax was implemented and a proportional corporate tax system was adopted. The tax reform was not only important for investment and technological innovation but also contributed to the high rate of savings for investment. These important reforms paved a way for the rapid economic growth.

With Japan's defeat after the war, the Japanese economy had three serious problems. First was expected to be huge unemployment. Second, the material losses of the war were 25 percent of national wealth, assets, and structures. Third, a rapid inflation developed. For the first problem, large-scale unemployment never actualized. To cope with above hardship, the Japanese government set forth two important goals during the years 1946–1948: (1) To accelerate the recovery of productive capacity in major industries, the government directly planned the growth of coal and steel industries in 1947 (so-called *priority production plan*). (2) To tame three-digit inflation, the government took drastic action (a "new yen" conversion) and direct control of prices and resource allocations. Despite every possible effort, the Japanese government could not combat inflation.

The Supreme Commander for the Allied Powers (*SCAP*) appointed the American banker Joseph Dodge to work in Japan in 1948. The government implemented his recommendation in 1949. The Dodge plan included a balanced budget, suspension of new loans from the Reconstruction Bank, and the reduction and abolition of subsidies. The exchange rate was set at $1=360 yen. As a result, the economy went into a severe deflationary spiral, but severe recession was averted by the special export demand created by the Korean War (June 1950).

1.3.2 Rapid Economic Growth Period

As a result of the San Francisco Peace Treaty in 1952, Japan became politically independent. Japan's miraculous rapid economic growth began in the early 1950s and lasted for nearly 20 years with an average annual growth rate of about 10 percent. The international background at the time provided for the rapid growth. Such factors included the low material prices that Japan needed to import, and the establishment of the *IMF* (1947) and *GATT* (1948) that promoted world progress.

We note some reasons for the rapid economic growth. (1) Since the beginning of the 1950s, foreign technology was introduced into Japan, bringing a high rate of continuous productivity increases. (2) The high saving rate of Japan provided sufficient funds to support the high investment rate. The Japanese tax and financial systems stressed the important role of the high rate of savings and its use; this effort was brought under the oversight of the Ministry of Finance (*MoF*) (called the Fiscal Investment and Loan Program, *FIL*). (3) The budgets for defense forces were small, and funds were directed to improve social infrastructures and government investment projects. (4) Japan's monetary and fiscal authorities made sound policy decisions during the period 1955–1964.

Japan initiated the following policies: (1) The Economic Planning Agency (*EPA*) has announced 5-year plans, setting the targets for the growth rate of *GNP* and its demand components. The plans were *indicative and more forecast-oriented* than directives. The proposed plans signaled the government's commitment to growth, giving confidence to industrial leaders. (2) The Ministry of International Trade and Industry (*MITI*) guided wise investment by setting target industries to identify sunrise industries and get them up and running quickly, including the allocation of foreign reserves for the purchase of capital equipment and raw materials, and the subsidization of loans for investment in structures and equipment. *MITI* also supplied administrative guidance (*gyosei shidou*) to regulate the speed of investment to avert excessive competition due to overcapacity. (3) Japan took a free trade policy; however, exceptions were the capital control against foreign capital and the infant industry protection. Japan became a member nation of *OECD* in 1964 (which was the year that the Tokyo Olympics were held), and decided to liberalize capital transactions. However, it was not until December 1980 that capital transactions became free in principle. The fixed exchange rate continued until the Nixon Shock or dollar shock (1971) and then the fixed exchange system moved in the float (1973).

1.3.3 Positive Effects (Economic Results)

The obvious economic results were greater increases of real *GDP*, per capita *GDP*, and real wages, to which the high growth rate of productivity largely contributed. Furthermore, the unemployment rate became extremely low at a little more than 1 percent (see Fig. 2.1). As a result, living conditions were improved, the middle class-consciousness greatly increased from 72.4 (1958) to 90.2 percent (1975), and the low class-consciousness fairly decreased. Social security system was improved. Livelihood protection was largely improved in terms of aid value. The Japanese universal medical care and the pension systems started in 1961. Infrastructure was also improved. Prime Minister Ikeda adapted "National Income Doubling Plan" (1960), which was an epoch in Japan as the first case of introduction of the infrastructure into the policy terminology. Every economic plan, since Ikeda's plan has followed the goal-setting of the infrastructure improvement by sector.

1.3.4 Negative Effects

Economic growth also brought various kinds of negative effects or distortions. Many infrastructures were rapidly improved during the rapid economic growth period; however, infrastructures fell behind production capital, and, among infrastructures, public assets related to daily life lagged further behind industrial infrastructures causing social imbalance. The negative results were more or less caused by social imbalance.

Concentration to metropolitan areas caused social maladies, pollution, congestion, and high cost of living on the one hand. On the other hand, depopulated areas faced a rapidly aging society and brought devastated places. To cope with the problem of depopulated areas, the government put the Act on Special Measures for Depopulated Areas in force and spent a large amount of money in the 1970s and again the 1980s. The population outflow slowed down, infrastructures were improved, but the problem remained.

The outstanding features of the environmental disruption process were (1) an extremely rapid expansion of heavy and chemical industries, (2) the progress in the degree of urbanization far in excess of demographic changes, and (3) the explosive boom in the mass consumption market, notably private cars. All of these caused woeful lags in the provision of complementary social overhead capital. The numbers of claims to pollution greatly increased. To cope with the problem, the government belatedly took various countermeasures; such was an enactment of the Basic Law for Environment Pollution Control (1967) and the establishment of the Environment Agency (1971). Then the government put the regulation into practice and fostered antipollution investment. As a result, the numbers of major claims to pollution greatly declined since the peak (1972) until 1995 (see Table 6.1 and Fig. 6.4).

Japan suffered from the high rate of inflation during the period from 1960 to the early 1980s. Inflation was more or less a cost of high economic growth, which was undesirable because of its adverse effects on income distribution. The population left behind by the advancing times were large numbers of low-income groups whose income would be at less than the government aid level. Differentials of government-assisted ratios among prefectures greatly increased and remained at its high level (see Fig. 6.5).

1.3.5 Moderate Economic Growth Period

The first oil crisis (1973) had a serious effect on the economy causing recession and an extraordinary price hike (see Fig. 2.2). The Japanese economy experienced negative growth for the first time in the postwar period. However, it was very successful in coping with the oil crisis. From the early 1980s Japan maintained price stability. Japan's trade surplus was positive after the first oil shock and enormously expanded from 1981 (see Fig. 2.7).

To cope with the huge trade deficit with the United States, the G5 agreed to further the dollar decline, under the Plaza Accord (1985). After this agreement, the Japanese yen greatly appreciated during the short period (from 237 to 159 yen to the dollar in terms of the monthly closing average during the 10-month period to July 1986) (see Fig. 2.7). This caused a serious shock to Japanese export industries and generated depression. The impact was so serious for these industries that the Bank of Japan reduced the official rate to the record low of 2.5 percent in February 1987 (until that time). This triggered an expansion of loans for speculative trading in shares and real estate. To cope with recession, the government initiated a huge emergency spending package.

Everything seemed to be going well. The share prices began to increase from the 1983 low and escalated in the following years. Real estate price also started to improve. Participants were involved in a buy-and-sell game, believing in those price increases (see Fig. 7.1). However this situation was unsustainable. Economic rationale could not explain the high transaction prices (see Table 7.1).

Average share prices rose almost 4.9 times (to the peak in 1989) from the 1982 year-end price. During the same period, average land prices of commercial and residential use in six major cities rose 5.0 and 2.9 times, respectively. The nationwide (all urban) land price grew by a factor of 1.7 from 1983 to 1991, equivalent to that of *GDP* (nominal) growth. Local land prices were not greatly affected in the bubble years (see Fig. 7.1). As a result, estimated capital gains in 1985 were enormous accounting for 601 trillion yen (1989) of corporate shares, and 1448 trillion yen (1990) of land.

During the bubble economy, we observed the following: (1) deterioration of asset and income distribution, particularly asset distribution, (2) large distortions of the resource allocation, and (3) serious housing problems.

1.3.6 Stagnation Period

The bubble economy burst in 1991. The average share price peaked in December 1989, fell 40 percent in 1990, declined until 1992, and then fluctuated to the bottom in 2002. On the other hand, the land price for commercial and residential use in six major cities increased until March 1990, and then continued to decline until 2005, which became 13 and 34 percent (1975 and 1983 levels), respectively against the peak.

From 1985 onward, capital gains of corporate shares greatly increased and then rapidly decreased in 1990 and 1992, and almost disappeared until 1998. The story was true of land also. Capital gains of land greatly increased from 1985 and then continuously decreased. The amount was possibly nil in the early 2000s (see Fig. 7.2 and Table 7.2).

There were serious consequences of the bubble burst. First, the transfer of factories abroad increased. The Japanese exchange rate to the dollar was 145 yen in 1990 and appreciated to 102 yen (annual average) in 1994. The dollar was shaken after the monetary and financial crises of the North American Foreign Trade Agreement (*NAFTA*), when the yen rate to dollar peaked at 79.75 yen in April 1995 (see Fig. 7.2). This resulted in serious difficulties for Japanese export industries and caused them to transfer their factories abroad, leading to the industrial hollowing-out of Japan.

Second was the huge nonperforming loans (*NPLs*) in Japanese banks. *NPLs* became conspicuous in 1993 and the amount increased until fiscal year (*FY*) 2001, peaking at 52.4 trillion yen at the end of March 2002. At that period, these amounts declined and the critical period nearly ended in *FY*2003, at which time the cumulative disposal from 1993 exceeded 100 trillion yen (see Fig. 8.2).

Third, the financial crisis (outstanding government bonds) was a result of the government policies. After the Plaza Accord, the national debt service payments ratio was about 20 percent. After the bubble burst, the dependency rate of *GB* issue to general accounts increased and exceeded 40 percent in 2003. As a result, *GB* outstanding amounted to 581 trillion yen of public bonds and some 26 trillion yen of the long-term borrowing (March-end 2010, government outlook) (see Fig. 8.3).

Neither the monetary policy of the low interest rate nor the fiscal policy of expanding public investment succeeded in bringing about economic recovery. The Koizumi administration took office in April 2001 carrying out the strong "structure reforms" policy, and the long-awaited economic recovery began in 2002.

1.4 Toward a Welfare-Oriented Society: Some Lessons from Rapid Economic Growth and the Bubble Economy

We now know that the theory of equating the growth of *GNP* with that of economic welfare is flawed. The *GNP* concept had measurement failures and conceptual limitations from the welfare viewpoint. Revising *GNP* or *GDP* formed *NNW* and the improved *GPI* from the viewpoint of welfare: subtracting nonwelfare items (pollution, military expenditure, and so on) and adding welfare items by monetary assessment (housekeeping work, voluntary activities, etc.). *NNW* has a weakness that it is not an index based on effective demand. Both categories of *GNP* and *NNW* are complementary, both of which are needed. The current *GDP* should be used for the practical purpose of judging market activity, but it is not a vitally important factor.

We give top priority to *GPI*, so that the concrete policy should be taken based on whether the policy is *GPI* enhancing or not. At the same time, important findings of happiness research should be taken into consideration. Examples are threshold income for the living satisfaction level, and substantial wellbeing benefits from institutional factors.

We can draw some lessons for relaxing or weakening the influence of the bubble. As George Soros (1998) mentioned, generating the bubble economy could not be avoided. The bubble may be guided by the nature of human beings: greediness. In this respect, government regulations and restrictions over the market would be effective to some extent, but may have limitations because lessons related to people and business reactions, business ethics, and the spirit of compliance are questions for the realm of psychology, morale, and philosophy. People's behavior depends on their value system. An important background may be on education in a broad sense, which is dealt with in the last chapter.

Our concluding comment considers lessons from the bubble economy from the viewpoint of a welfare-oriented society. The above-mentioned costs of the bubble during and after the bubble were all deteriorating effect on welfare-oriented society. Those costs were serious and extremely huge. For a whole society, the bubble economy was not a zero-sum game but everyone lost. Considering these sad situations, we offer two kinds of advice. First is to initiate policy controls and market regulations, which may relax or weaken the effect of the bubble. Second is to set a safety net for the people who need help sustaining their living standards or are victims of economic fluctuations or disaster. In this respect, we share Rawl's (1971) idea in a broad sense.

1.5 Quality of Life in the Mature Society

Our methodological standpoint to construct a welfare-oriented society is to use *GPI*. Both *GDP* and *GPI* are complementary, but we give top priority to *GPI*. We consider a mature society as a society in advanced countries with more than *GNP* per capita in *ppp* (purchasing power parity) 1995 of about US$10,000.

Our systemic design of this society is still in an infancy stage and has three important properties. First is the safety net. Society prepares for the social security such as livelihood protection, medical insurance, and pension. The government serves a major function of this safety net, but the company and the household also serve part of the function. Second is a safe society, which has the following properties: low crime rate, no pollution, small numbers of traffic accident, safe food, and so on. Third is keeping social balance between privately produced goods and services and those of the public sector.

The most important foundation on which to build our ideal society may be education in a broad sense that includes social, family, and school education. The living satisfaction level highly depends on individual aspirations, and this desire is insatiable without a moderate sense of life (a life balance between the material and the other), which relates to the philosophy of life or the way of life.

1.6 The Plan

This book is organized as follows. The first chapter outlines my intention and gives a sketch of the book. Overview of postwar Japan includes the political and the economic landscapes; in addition, the economic landscape by period is examined. We propose a welfare-oriented society as an outcome to rapid economic growth and the bubble economy. This leads to our goal, "quality of life in the mature society." Chapter 2 presents historical changes in the Japanese economy from various aspects using figures and tables that will give the reader an overview of the Japanese economy during the postwar period. This includes labor force status (unemployment), price increases, income and income distribution, structural changes in the economy, and international concern.

Chapter 3 deals with above-mentioned subject, "Recovery Period." We examine "Rapid Economic Growth Period," "Positive Effects," and "Negative Effects," in Chapters 4, 5, and 6, respectively. Chapters 7 and 8 mostly correspond to "Moderate Economic Growth Period," and "Stagnation Period," respectively. Chapter 9 corresponds to "Toward a Welfare-Oriented Society: Some Lessons from the Rapid Economic Growth and the Bubble Economy."

In Chapters 10 and 11, we look at some of the important economic issues for Japan that may closely relate to a welfare-oriented society. Chapter 10 deals with an important current issue: income distribution, asset distribution, and the relative share of income. We observe changes in the Japanese income distribution during the postwar period and discuss where Japan ranks internationally. We analyze asset distribution by distinguishing between financial assets and physical assets and present some properties of asset distribution. Then we discuss the matter of the relative share of income: estimates, properties, and the theoretical explanation. Chapter 11 looks at Japanese household structure and the pension issue. In Chapter 10, we examine the importance of the effect of the demographic change on income distribution, which also has a close relationship with the pension issue. For the pension issue, we deal with its brief history, serious concerns, and solutions.

Chapter 12 summarizes the quality of life as the ultimate lesson of this research. We briefly outline a proposal for a basic design toward achieving a high satisfaction level society. That is, the "quality of life in the mature society" is the direction in which all policies should lead.

Note

1. We now use *GDP* as the conventional measurement. After World War II, Gross National Product (*GNP*) was used for many years, so we use this category in most of the chapters. However, the same discussion holds true for *GDP*. *GNP* is not an appropriate measure for viewing domestic economic activity when the country has a relatively large amount of net factor income received from abroad. The United States and Japan changed their reporting forms to *GDP* from *GNP* in 1991. In the 93 System of National Accounts (93 *SNA*) proposed by the United Nations in 1993, importance was given to the form of *GDP* and *GNI* (gross national income) was adopted instead of *GNP*. Japan replaced the former system with this in October 2000. *GNI* and *GNP* are the same amount in nominal terms, but are different in real terms. In real terms, *GNI* includes trading gains but *GNP* does not. Trading gains are economic gains that are brought by the change of the terms of trade expressed by "export price index/import price index."

Chapter 2
Historical Changes of the Japanese Economy

This chapter explains historical changes of the Japanese economy using statistical data. After World War II, the Japanese economy experienced rapid changes and remarkable progress, although it also experienced the bubble economy and prolonged stagnation. In an attempt to understand the historical changes, we discuss the labor force status, price increases, income and income distribution, structural changes, and international concern using figures and tables.

2.1 Postwar Labor Force Status

After World War II a high unemployment rate was expected due to demobilized troops, laid-off workers from military production, and repatriates from abroad, but large-scale unemployment never really materialized. We explain the reason in Chapter 3, Section 3.4. Figure 2.1 shows the labor force status for 1953–2008, age 15 years and older. The Japanese definition of unemployed person is based on the International Labor Organization (*ILO*) standard, which is comparable with the standardized unemployment rate calculated by *OECD* for 27 countries.

Japan's postwar labor force status has the following characteristics: First is the unemployment rate, which was very low particularly during the period 1961–1974, the peak was 5.4 percent in 2002, 1.4 and 1.1 percent. After the first oil shock, the rate gradually increased and the peak was 5.4 percent in 2002. Corresponding to this change, the number of unemployed persons increased, and the peak was 3.59 million in 2002. The unemployment rate for males was higher than for females, except for the periods 1961–1967 and 1984–1995, although the differences were small. Compared with the *OECD* average of the standardized unemployment rate (5.6 percent, 2007), the Japanese unemployment rate was still in the lower group at 3.9 percent (2007). (*OECD*, Statistics Portal (http://www.oecd.org).)

Second is the labor force participation rate. The rate for males has gradually decreased from 86.4 (1953) to 72.8 percent (2008). Females showed a declining trend from 56.7 (1955) to 45.7 percent (1975), and then kept more or less a steady level. The gap between the male and female rates was enormous at 35.7 percentage points in 1975, and gradually declined to about 20 percentage points in 2008.

M. Iyoda, *Postwar Japanese Economy*, DOI 10.1007/978-1-4419-6332-1_2,
© Springer Science+Business Media, LLC 2010

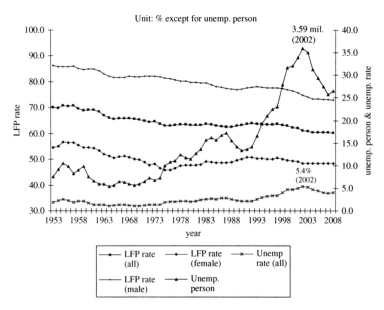

Fig. 2.1 Labor force status (whole Japan).
Source: (www.stat.go.jp/roudou/longtime/zuhyo/Ito2.xls), Historical data 2
Note: 1. *LFP* rate = labor force participation rate defined as (labor force/population of 15 years old or more); Unemp. person = unemployed person (in hundred thousand); Unemp. rate = unemployment rate; 2. Okinawa prefecture is not included in the figures until 1972

Japanese females are still largely engaged in housekeeping (some 55 percent of nonlabor force of females, 2008).

Third are some characteristics of the labor force status in recent 10 years. (see SB of MIAC (d), 2007, Overview of the Results). (1) The male unemployment rate is higher than the female. (2) A breakdown of the unemployment rate by sex and age group shows rates peaking in the 15–24 age groups for both sexes. Compared with the unemployment rate by sex during the period of 1997–2007, this age group of males was 9.7 percent versus the average of males at 4.7 percent; females were 7.8 percent against the average at 4.3 percent. (3) The number of young unemployed persons in the 15–34 age group was 1.17 million and that of Not in Education, Employment, or Training (*NEET*s)[1] by the same age group was 0.62 million. The peak was 1.68 and 0.64 million, respectively (both in 2002). (4) The unemployment rate difference by region was large. The unemployment rate for all Japan was 4.5 percent on the average for 1997–2007. The high rate regions among ten regions were Kinki (the second business center region of Japan, 5.5), Hokkaido (northern island, 5.4), and Kyushu (southern island, 5.2). The lowest regions during the same period were Tokai (the center of the main island facing the Pacific Ocean, 3.5) and Hokuriku (the center of the main island facing the Japan Sea, 3.5).[2]

2.2 Price Increase

During the recovery period after World War II, inflation ran into three digits. The government made a desperate effort to tame inflation, but without success until the introduction of the Dodge Plan (1949). We examine this matter more closely in Chapter 3.

Figure 2.2 shows the rate of increase of The *CPI* (consumer price index) and *DCPI* (domestic corporate price index) since 1955. *CPI* accelerated during high economic growth and escalated after the first oil crisis in 1973 (23.2 percent in 1974). However, since the early 1980s, Japanese *CPI* slowed down until 2007, which made inflation a less important matter. However, Japan has been involved in a serious deflationary spiral since the early 1990s. But reflecting food material and energy prices, the CPI increased in the last quarter of 2007.

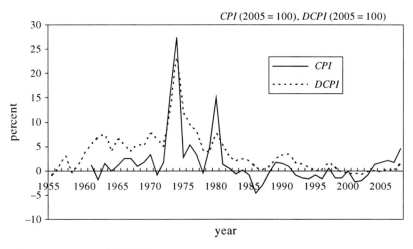

Fig. 2.2 Price increase (1955–2008).
Sources: CAO of GoJ (2009), Long-Term Economic Statistics (downloaded from Japanese ed.)
Note: *CPI* (consumer price index, Y2005=100); *DCPI* (domestic corporate price index, Y2005=100)

Figure 2.2 also shows *DCPI*, which is a renamed index (with improvement) of the former Japanese *WPI* (wholesale price index). The *DCPI* had two spikes, each of which was affected by the respective oil shocks of 1973 and 1979. Except for the period (1973–1980) affected by the oil crises, the price increase was not large; in particular, from the early 1980s until 2003, most of the years saw negative growth. This was greatly affected by the following factors: Japanese manufacturing industries had strong competitive power in the world market, which allowed Japan to have a great trade surplus. The trade surplus also spurred the Japanese exchange rate of yen upward to the US dollar and other currencies. Japan highly depends on the import of raw materials, particularly energy-related materials. Since the early 1980s, the price of primary goods in general slowed down and stabilized until 2003. All of these factors contributed to the negative growth rate of the Japanese *DCPI*. However, reflecting price increases of petroleum, coal products, and nonferrous metals, and so on, this rate has been increasing since 2004 and accelerated in the summer of 2008.

2.3 Income and Income Distribution

2.3.1 Income

Figure 2.3 shows the per capita *GDP* growth rate during the past half century since 1955. The Japanese per capita *GDP* index in real terms showed remarkable growth in terms of yen. It increased by an approximate factor of eight during the past half century—4 times in the first 20 years until 1975, and 2 times in the period after 1975, with the final 2 times occurring in the last 30 years. However, the growth might be overestimated in terms of US dollars due to the steep appreciation of the yen, particularly in 1990 and 1995. Despite that, the index of per capita *GDP* in real terms (1955=100) increased 31 percent to 712 (1995) from 543 (1985), while per capita *GDP* in terms of US dollars greatly increased to 41,843 from 11,250 during the same period.[3] (see Fig. 2.7 for the exchange rate of yen to the US dollar.) Note that a simple international comparison may lead to misunderstanding the real situation.

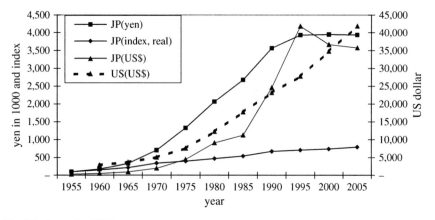

Fig. 2.3 Per capita *GDP*.
Sources: Japan Statistical Association (2006), Vol. 1, T3-1, *GDP* deflator (p. 235). CAO of GoJ (2006), per capita *GDP* (p. 434), exchange rate (p. 446); DNA of ESRI, CAO (a) (2008), *GDP* deflator (p. 141). Council of Economic Advisors (2008), TB-31, current
Notes: 1. Data are taken once in every 5 years; 2. JP (yen) = per capita *GDP* at current prices; 3. Per capita *GDP* (US$) is calculated by the central-rate average exchange rate; 4. JP (index, real) = Japanese per capita *GDP* index at constant prices (yen, 1955=100). We obtained JP (real) by using *GDP* deflator of 68 *SNA* with extension from 1999–2005; 5. US (US$) = US per capita *GDP* at current prices

2.3.2 Income Distribution

There are several Gini coefficients of income distribution depending on the data. Available data vary from annual to once every 3 years and from a short- to long-time series. However, in observing the trend, most Gini coefficients[4] show similar properties (see QLPB of EPA, 1999, Figure 3-2-1). Figure 2.4 shows two kinds of Japanese Gini coefficients, which are in the highest and the lowest groups. Major differences are caused by the different coverage: Gini (1) includes workers' households with two or more persons; Gini (2) includes all types of households (including one-person households). Furthermore, Gini (1) includes payment of public pension but excludes insurance benefits and retirement payments; Gini (2) (before redistribution of income) includes insurance benefits and retirement payments, but excludes payment of public pension.

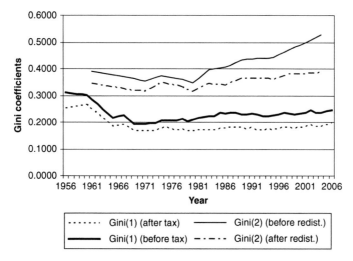

Fig. 2.4 Income distribution.
Sources: CAO (2007), p. 261 for Gini (1) (calculated from *Family Income and Expenditure Survey*). Survey Section of PDMS, MHLW (–2005 survey, Table 2 or 3) for Gini (2) (calculated from *Income Distribution Survey*)
Notes: Gini (1) includes workers' households (with two persons or more). Gini (2) includes all types of households (including one-person households)

Japanese income distribution showed a strong equalizing trend in the 1960s, particularly with Gini (1). Since the 1980s, however, it has been gradually deteriorating up to present day. International comparison of income distribution is difficult, and the result is divided by which datum is used for comparison. CAO of GoJ (2007, p. 315) shows that the (equivalence-based) Gini coefficient of Japan based on household disposal income is slightly higher than that of the average of *OECD* nations.

In recent years, income distribution has become a political as well as an economic issue in Japan. There have been heated discussions regarding the cause of deterioration in income distribution since 1990 and how Japanese income distribution ranks internationally. We examine these matters in Chapter 10.

2.4 Structural Changes

2.4.1 Production by Industry

Figure 2.5 shows structural changes of production by industry. In 1952, the tertiary industry produced 45.6 percent of total production, the secondary industry 30.7 percent, and the primary industry 22.9 percent. Since then, there has been a sharp contraction of the primary industry and a great expansion of the tertiary industry. In 2005, the tertiary industry produced the majority percentage of 74.8, the secondary industry 28.0 percent, but the primary industry only 1.5 percent. The peak of the secondary industry was 44.5 percent in 1970.

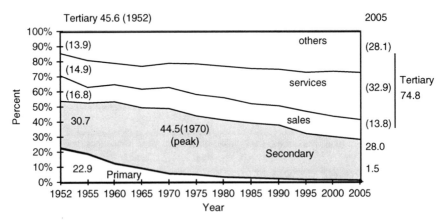

Fig. 2.5 Structural changes of production by industry.
Source: DNA of ESRI, CAO (a) (2008)
Note: *GDP* by major industry at current prices. Percentages are before adjustment of "taxes and duties on imports" less "consumption taxes for gross capital formation and imputed bank service charges." Therefore, the total average for 1955–2005 is 103.5

2.4.2 Labor Force by Industry and Status in Employment

Similar changes are observed in Figure 2.6a that shows structural changes of the labor force by industry.[5] In 1950, 29.6 percent of the labor force worked in the tertiary industry, 21.8 percent in the secondary industry, and nearly a half of the labor force (48.5 percent) in the primary industry. The majority labor force (67.3 percent) now works in the tertiary industry, 25.9 percent in the secondary industry, and again a small 4.8 percent labor force is in the primary industry (2005). The peak of the secondary industry was 34.1 percent in 1975.

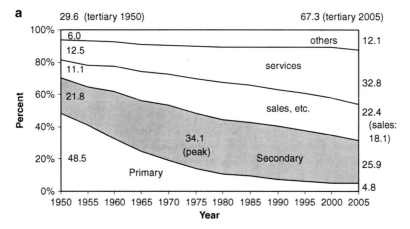

Fig. 2.6a Structural changes of labor force by industry.
Source: SB of MIAC (f) (2008), Table 3 for 1950–2000; SB of MIAC (h) (2009), Table 1 for 2005
Notes: 2005 data follows the revision of the Japan Standard Industry Classification, but subgroups of the tertiary industry do not. The current international industry classification includes "mining" in the primary industry; however, the Japanese classification continues to classify this in the secondary industry. The percentage distribution of mining in Japan was very low and only 0.1 in terms of both production and the labor force (2000 and 2005). Industries unable to classify were 1.9 percent in 2005.
Industry classification in figures. Primary: agriculture, fishery, and forestry. Secondary: mining, construction, and manufacturing. Tertiary: sales, and so on (wholesale, retail trade, and eating and drinking places), services (service activities, government services, private nonprofit services to households), and others (electricity, gas, and water supply, finance and insurance, real estate, transport and communications)

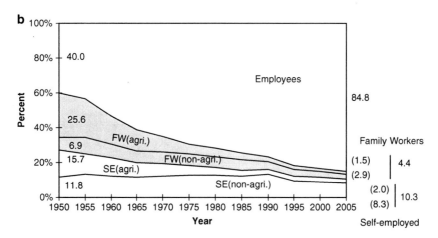

Fig. 2.6b Structural changes of labor (by Status in Employment).
Sources: SB of MCA (c) (–2001); SB of MIAC (d) (2006)
Note: FW (family workers); SE (self-employed)

These well-known phenomena are explained by the Petty-Clark Law.[6] Applying this law, we consider that economic development is the process of the structural change; whereby there is the shift of major industry. That is, economic growth moves from the agricultural society to the industrial society, and then to the postindustrial society, the last of which we may call the information society.

Figure 2.6b shows structural changes of the labor force (by status in employment). In 1950, 40 percent of the labor force was employees and the majority labor force (60 percent) worked for the self-employed businesses as the self-employed or family workers. In particular, 41.3 percent were working for agriculture. Since then, there has been a sharp decline in the number of the self-employed people and family workers. Conversely, there has been a steady increase in the number of employees. In 2005, about 85 percent of the labor force were employees and only 15 percent were the self-employed and family workers; for agriculture, those percentages are only 3.6 percent.

According to data since 1950 (or 1952), we observed structural changes in production by industry, labor force by industry, and by status in employment. Structural changes were drastic and in general followed the Petty-Clark Law. The turning point in the Japanese secondary industry seemed to be in the first half of the 1970s. Note that those three Figs. 2.5, 2.6a, b are not based on yearly data but 5-year data.

By using these figures, we compare the magnitude and speed of the structural change between 1950 and 1975 and between 1975 and 2005. Table 2.1 shows the contraction magnitude and speed between these periods. The contraction of production and labor force in primary industry was very large throughout the whole observation period; however, these changes during the period up to 1975 were greater than those after the 1975 period by about 1.5 times. The contraction speed of the self-employed labor force between those two periods was more or less similar, but in agriculture the speed upto the 1975 period was larger than that after

Table 2.1 Contraction magnitudes and speed between 1950 and 1975 and between 1975 and 2005

Magnitude and speed	Percentage distribution			Annual change, %		Ratio
	1950	1975	2005	(a/b)/25	(b/c)/30	d/e
Items	(a)	(b)	(c)	(d)	(e)	(f)
Production in primary industry	22.9[a]	5.5	1.5	18.1[b]	12.2	1.48
Labor force in primary industry	48.5	13.8	4.8	14.1	9.6	1.47
Self-employed labor force	60.0	30.1	15.2	8.0	6.6	1.21
of which in agriculture	41.3	11.3	3.5	14.6	10.8	1.36
Self-employed sector (product)[c]	43.0	15.3	–	11.2	–	–
of which in agriculture	24.0	4.6	–	20.9	–	–

[a] 1952 value. [b] (a/b)/23. [c] Percent in *NNP* (net National Product)
Sources: Figures 2.5, 2.6a, b; Iyoda (1984), Table 3 for self-employed sector (product)

the 1975 period by 1.36 times. Contraction magnitudes and speed of product in the self-employed sector, particularly in agriculture, were far greater. By observation, we confirmed that rapid economic growth was accompanied by rapid structural changes.

2.5 International Concern

2.5.1 Exchange Rate

After the World War II period, the Japanese government was not successful in taming inflation. To combat inflation, the government put the Dodge plan in force in 1949. The exchange rate was set at $1 = 360$ yen, under which the Japanese economy had remarkable economic growth for some two decades. (see Chapter 3 for the Dodge plan). Figure 2.7 shows the exchange rate and the trade balance. It was after the Nixon Shock (1971) that the exchange rate became float. Since then, the Japanese exchange rate (to dollar) fluctuated, but had a strong tendency of up-valuation until the middle 1990s, then being kept at a highly appreciated level.

By observation, we found two greater appreciation periods of the yen (1971–1978 and 1985–1995), of which the first started from the Nixon Shock and the second from the Plaza Accord. Facing the US gold reserve shortage, then President Nixon announced suspension of convertibility of the dollar into gold on August 15, 1971. This brought a great shock to the world economy. As a result, the fixed exchange rate system moved in the float (see Chapter 4, Section 4.3 for the details). The world's leading financial ministers of the G5 had a conference and agreed to further the dollar decline for solving the US trade imbalances in September 1985. This was the so-called Plaza Accord. (See Chapter 7, Section 7.2 for the detail.)

2.5.2 Trade Balance and Foreign Investment

Figure 2.7 also shows the Japanese trade balance. From the middle 1960s onward, the trade balance was in surplus. Despite the up-valuation of the yen, Japan had huge trade surplus in particular from 1981. This phenomenon seems to be against the exchange rate theory. We deal with this matter in Chapter 7, Section 7.2.

Figure 2.8 shows the exchange rate and foreign direct investment. Japan became a member nation of *OECD* in 1964. Japan decided to liberalize capital transactions, however, it was in December 1980 that capital transaction became free in principle. Reflecting the trade surplus since 1981, Japan's foreign direct investment increased. After the Plaza Accord, it accelerated until 1990 reflecting the sharp appreciation of the yen. After bursting the bubble, it decreased to 1993; however, after that there was an increasing trend to 2008, though the volume oscillated considerably. On the

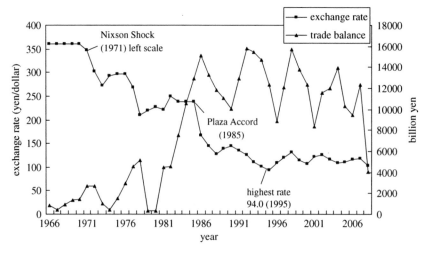

Fig. 2.7 Trade balance and exchange rate.
Sources: CAO of GoJ (2009, Japanese ed.), Long-Term Economic Statistics (home page: www5.
cao.gov.jp/j-j/wp/wp-je08/08.html)
Note: The exchange rate is the mid-month average for the central inter-bank spot rate. It is a simple
average of monthly figure after 2003 and business day average before 2002

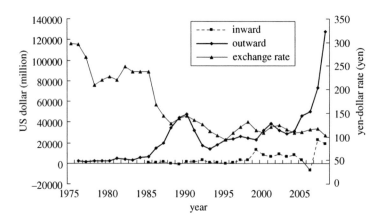

Fig. 2.8 Exchange Rate and Foreign Investment.
Sources: RSD of BoJ (b) (2009), foreign exchange rates (central rate average) for 1975–2008
and direct investments for 1996–2007; RSD of BoJ (c) (1977, 1986, 1991), direct investments for
1976–1990; International Department of BoJ (1996, 2000), direct investments for 1991–1995
Note: Direct investment (inward and outward) in terms of yen was converted by the exchange rate
(central rate average) into US dollars for 1976–1984 and 1996–2008

other hand, inward foreign direct investment had been small. It increased from 1999,
which is still small compared with outward direct investment. "In Japan's case, this
is an indication that in many industries restrictions are imposed on investment from
foreign companies." (see CAO of GoJ, 2003–2004, p. 199.)[7]

Notes

1. In the Labor Force Survey, the term "young unemployed persons" is used to refer to unemployed persons in the 15–34 age group, and *NEETs* is used to refer to those in 15–34 age group not in the labor force and not engaged in housekeeping or attending school.
2. Calculated from SB of MCA (c) (1997–2001), Table 29 and SB of MIAC (d) (2002–2007), Table 29.
3. Nominal values are inflated by the price increases and sometimes overestimated by the fluctuating exchange rate. The US per capita *GDP* at current prices is also inflated by the price increase. During the period from 1985 to 1995, the Japanese price was stabilized (the annual averaged increase was 1.2 percent).
4. Gini coefficient is defined as a coefficient which shows the degree of inequality in a frequency distribution. It means that the higher the Gini coefficient the greater the degree of inequality.
5. If we compare Fig. 2.5 with Fig. 26a, we will be able to find relative productivity of the industry. For example, "others" of the tertiary industry consist of highly productive industries, while "sales" of the tertiary and the primary industry are low productivity industries.
6. British economist William Petty (1623–1687) (1690) observed that, as a rule of thumb, returns would increase in the following order: agriculture, production industry, and then commerce. Another British Economist Colin G. Clark (1905–1989) (1940) explained by the statistical data that, in the course of economic growth, the occupational structure shifts from primary (agriculture) to secondary (production), and then to tertiary industries.
7. For example, the Code of Liberalization of Capital Movement of the *OECD* has reservations on the following eight industries: maritime transport, air transport, agriculture, forestry, fisheries, mining, oil, leather and leather product manufacturing (loc. cit.). Also, see Mogbel (2005) for the outward and inward direct investment of Japan.

Chapter 3
Recovery Period (Reforms, Social and Political Changes, and Economic Policy)

After World War II, the Allied Occupation Force headed by General Douglas MacArthur governed Japan. The General Head Quarter (*GHQ*) imposed three major economic reforms aimed at democratizing Japan politically and economically. The occupation policy at first was extremely severe; however, the world political situation was greatly changing as a result of the Cold War. Reflecting these situations, this policy was gradually relaxed. However, economic reforms and social and political changes under the occupation made a great contribution in a broad sense for the rapid economic growth thereafter.

This chapter discusses the occupation, reforms, social and political changes, and the government policy during this period.

3.1 The Occupation

From 1945 to 1952 Japan was occupied by the allied forces under the command of General Douglas MacArthur, the Supreme Commander for the Allied Powers (*SCAP*). Recognizing the existence of the Japanese government, the occupation ruled indirectly and the Japanese bureaucratic system[1] was preserved. MacArthur's primary objectives for Japan were to see its demilitarization and democratization. The US Initial Post-Surrender Policy had been drawn up in Washington. The tone of the reforms was on the whole extremely severe. Demilitarization was achieved through the suspension of military production, a ban on fleet and aircraft facilities, and restrictions on heavy industries and merchant vessels (see Hsu 1999, p. 345, Nakamura 1995, pp. 24–5).

Economic democratization consisted mainly of three reforms: antitrust measures, land reform, and labor reform. Other areas for democratization were the education system and the political system, including a new constitution for Japan. These are explained below.

World political background was changing during the occupation. In October 1947, the Cominform[2] was organized by the Soviet Union and East European Countries. In 1948, the blockade of Berlin by the Soviet Union was countered by

M. Iyoda, *Postwar Japanese Economy*, DOI 10.1007/978-1-4419-6332-1_3,
© Springer Science+Business Media, LLC 2010

a massive US airlift. The People's Republic of China was proclaimed with Mao Zedong as its chairman in October 1949. Reflecting these political movements the Cold War began with two blocks, one headed by the United States and the other by the USSR, (Union of Soviet Socialist Republics) fiercely confronting each other. With the intensification of the Cold War, the US policy shifted from one of democratization and reform to the rebuilding of Japan as a strong ally. As a result, some of the reforms and changes were diluted and relaxed. One notable change was the military aspect: a Police Reserve Force was set up at MacArthur's direction in 1950, leading to the establishment of Self-Defense Forces in 1954.

Finally, as a result of the San Francisco Peace Treaty, Japan became independent in April 1952. The Japan–US Security Treaty was set up at the same time. At this point, Japan was fully independent again.

3.2 Important Reforms

3.2.1 Antitrust Measures

During the occupation, the *GHQ* imposed three antitrust measures. First was dissolution of the *zaibatsu*.[3] The zaibatsu consists of groups of large companies across different industries controlled by family-owned holding companies. The *GHQ* considered that "the purpose of zaibatsu dissolution…is to destroy Japan's military power both psychologically and institutionally" (Nakamura 1995, p. 25). Zaibatsu groups held about 40 percent of the total shares of stock in 1946. The Holding Company Liquidation Commission (*HCLC*) was established as an enforcement body (in 1946) to oversee the dissolution of zaibatsus by selling to the public the shares owned by these holding companies. The zaibatsu leaders, including the members of the founding families, were purged and were prohibited from further activities in the financial world (Nakamura 1995, p. 26). Of the 83 companies initially appointed as Zaibatsu holding companies, 28 companies were actually dissolved (HCLC 1973, Part 2, Chapter 2; Harada and Kosai 1987, pp. 110–111).

The second antitrust measure was enactment of the Anti-Monopoly Law (1947), which was intended to maintain competition. The law was modeled on American antitrust laws, which banned trusts, cartels, as well as holding companies.[4] This became a basic principle of the postwar Japanese economy; however, after two revisions in 1949 and 1953, the law was greatly relaxed. The third measure was the Elimination of Excessive Concentration of Economic Power Law (1947), which was intended to break up monopolistic companies. Of the 325 large companies targeted, only 18 companies were broken up, including Nippon Steel, Mitsui Mining, and Mitsubishi Mining (HCLC 1973, Part 2, Chapter 6; Ito 1992, p. 179; Nakamura 1995, p. 27). It became an interim measure. Reflecting the deepening of the Cold War,[5] the GHQ's policy changed from one of weakening the Japanese economy to helping Japan to become a strong ally.

As a result, these measures fostered market competition, promoted vigorous investment demand, and enhanced consumer welfare.

3.2.2 Land Reform

The second step in Japan's economic democratization was the land reform imposed during the years 1946–1950. Properties were actually confiscated with little compensation to landlords and resold to tenant farmers at bargain prices. Absentee landlords (who were not residing on their own land areas) were not allowed to hold any land; nonabsentee landlords residing in the rural villages were allowed to hold one *cho* or 2.45 acres (approximately one hectare). As a result of the land reform, the cultivated percentage of farmland by tenant farmers greatly declined from 46 (1946) to 10 (1950). (Nakamura 1995, Table 2.2, p. 29.)

The land reform was not intended as confiscation at first, but it actually became confiscation. The landlord received 978 yen with bonds (for rice fields) and 577 yen (for fields other than rice) per one *tan* or 0.245 acre (approximately 10 ares), but the received value was equivalent to only 7 percent of the harvest value, which was caused by the extremely high rate of inflation in 1947–1948. On the other hand, tenant farmers paid 757 yen (for rice field) and 466 yen (for field) per 1 *tan* or 0.245 acre (Harada and Kosai 1987, p. 106).

As a result, land reform created a middle class as agricultural production increased rapidly. This in turn contributed to income equality and political stability in the agricultural sector in Japan as private ownership was supported. On the other hand, the land reform prevented scale merit farming, which became a drawback in later years as economic growth continued.

3.2.3 Labor Reform

For labor reform, the *GHQ* imposed three important laws. First was the Labor Union Law (1946), by which workers were granted the rights to organize in unions and to engage in collective bargaining. Second was the Labor Relations Adjustment Law (1946), which established the machinery for bargaining: national and 46 local boards to mediate and arbitrate disputes. Last was the Labor Standards Law (1947), which set the working conditions and terms of work based on International Labor Organization conventions. The terms included introduction of the 8-h work day and holiday systems, limitation on women and minors' employment, and establishment of work-related injury compensation.

As a result, labor unions spread quickly. Social democrats and other moderate left-wing organizers revived the prewar Sodomei, or Japan Confederation of Trade Unions, in August 1946. The All Japan Congress of Industrial Unions (Sanbetsu), linking with the Communist Party, was established in August 1948. The Sanbetsu, being dominant at first, stood in opposition to the Sodomei. Reflecting the increase in the number of labor unions, the unionized percentage of workers jumped from 3.2 (1945) to 41.5 (1946), then to 53.0 (1948). Unionization of workers increased the number of strikes and labor–management conflicts. In 1948, they accounted for up to 913 strikes and more than 2.6 million workers were involved (Ito 1992, p. 55). Collective bargaining between labor and management was the first experience causing chaotic situations. Furthermore, general working conditions of workers were not stabilized due to extremely high rate of inflation in those years.

The occupation forces were initially sympathetic to the activities of the left-wing unions and sought to allow them full freedom in the name of democratization (Nakamura 1995, pp. 30–31). The *GHQ* modified its policies as the Cold War intensified. The *GHQ* ordered the cancellation of the planned general strike of February 1, 1947. The *GHQ* issued a political order depriving government employees of the right to strike (August 1948) and acquiesced in political firings, the "red purge"[6] in 1949. These actions were a result of the shadow cast by the Cold War. Due to the change in the occupation policy, Sanbetsu's dominance began to wane. The Japan General Council of Trade Unions (Sohyo) was formed against the left-wing socialist and communist movement in July 1950, but it too became increasingly leftist. (See Nakmura 1995, pp. 30–31; Koshiro 2000, Chapter 1, pp. 20–21, and pp. 32–35).

Japan's union movement grew stronger and made rapid progress through labor disputes, gaining an increase in real wages and better working conditions. As a result of these negotiations, the Japanese style of labor management was established with lifetime employment, and the introduction of a seniority wage system and enterprise unions (unions organized by each enterprise).[7] In the 1960s, the cooperative labor–management relationship emerged nationwide.

3.2.4 Tax Reform

Finally, we deal with a tax reform, which was not imposed by the GHQ; however, it was not only important for investment and technological innovation but also contributed to the high rate of savings for investment. A tax reform was implemented during the occupation period in accordance with the recommendations of the Shoup Mission led by American economist Carol Shoup in 1949 and 1950. After the implementation of the initial reform, however, various additions and revisions were made (see Nakamura 1995, pp. 46–48; Komiya 1975, Chapter 3 for details).

3.2.4.1 Income Tax

A system based on a comprehensive income tax was implemented, in which all categories of income were added together and were subject to the same tax rate. The progressive income tax was applied to the income. After this, however, to increase individual savings, various kinds of preferential taxes on assets income were introduced. A separate tax on interest (1951) and dividend income (1952) was instituted. In 1953, the income exemption from the transfer of securities was implemented. The tax exemption for interest income from various types of privileged savings (small-saver savings, postal savings, national and local bonds, and so on.) had been enacted during wartime, while the tax exemptions increased four times from 1950 to 1965. This nontax plan was abolished in the 1988 tax reform.

3.2.4.2 Corporate Tax

A proportional corporate tax system was adopted. Shoup called for the elimination of preferential tax treatment given to special interests and industries. However, particular emphasis was placed on special tax measures for the promotion of plant and equipment investment and exports. Preferential tax treatments were implemented in the early 1950s: examples were the abolition of the tax on the reserves of nonfamily business firms, an introduction of the special depreciation system for important machinery, a tax exemption on key products, tax reductions on export income, and a system of reserves against export losses.

During the recovery period, Japan had important four reforms: antitrust measures and land, labor, and tax reform. Although the *GHQ* imposed these first three reforms with the aim to democratize Japan politically and economically, these reforms paved a way for the rapid economic growth hereafter. Systemic reforms brought competitive economy (economic efficiency) to Japan.

3.3 Other Drastic Social and Political Changes

There were several important social and political changes at this time. Among others, we discuss the education and the political systems.

3.3.1 Education System

The Japanese education system in prewar days was revised occasionally; however, since 1907, a 6-year elementary school education was compulsory, with boys and girls taught separate courses. For boys, there was a 5-year middle school, a 3-year high school, and a 3-year university. For girls, there was a 5-year high school and a 3-year senior high school.

After World War II, Japan adopted the American model for its education system and introduced a 6-3-3-4 system. That is, a 9-year compulsory school education, which consists of 6 years of elementary school and 3 years of junior high school. Further education is optional with a 3-year senior high school education, then a 2-year junior college or 4-year college or university education. This was a unitary system of schools. Education was open to everyone at each stage according to his or her abilities. This basically contrasted to the prewar dual system where schools were separated between the upper class and the general public. The postwar unitary system of schools contributed to equal educational opportunities but brought with it a fiercely competitive entrance examination. In 1962, a 5-year technical college was introduced later for junior high school graduates in response to the increasing industrial demand for junior engineers. Junior colleges were established in 1950 and perpetualized in 1964. The special training system was established in 1976. The majority of students are involved in curriculums in medical science, technology, and home economics.

Coeducation was introduced at the compulsory stage, but an option was allowed for separate classes by sex for higher education.

3.3.2 Political System

The Japanese political system resembles the British system. The emperor is considered to be a symbol of the nation rather than simply a head of the state. There are two houses in the Diet (Parliament): the House of Representatives (Lower House) and the House of Councillors (Upper House). The head of government, the prime minister, is elected in the Diet and a majority of cabinet members must be members of the Diet. Members of both houses are elected; the methods of election and the lengths of terms differ between the houses.[8]

Guided by the *GHQ*, Japan established a new Constitution of Japan (1947) instead of the prewar Imperial Constitution. Military forces were permanently banned by Article 9 of the constitution. Self-defense forces were established later to counter the communist threat during the Cold War in 1954. Women obtained their voting rights, so that all Japanese adults aged 20 years and older had voting rights. The election of the members of the House of Councillors (Upper House) was introduced whereas previously it had consisted of the privileged and the upper ruling classes.

These systemic changes in education and politics strongly transformed Japan into a democratic society. The power elite was replaced by the young generation. Through social and political changes, Japanese have subconsciously limited the US culture. The military industry lost its base as a result of the new constitution and the antitrust measures destroyed rent-seeking movement[9] by industry.

3.4 Economic Policy (1945–1950)

There were many victims of the war. Casualties accounted for more than 2.5 million, including the wounded and missing. If we added Japanese casualties overseas, the total approached 3 million (Nakamura 1995, p. 15). Massive casualties consisted of soldiers, sailors and civilians.

With Japan's defeat, the Japanese economy had three serious problems. First was the expected huge unemployment from demobilized troops, workers from military production, and repatriates from abroad. However, large-scale unemployment never materialized. Many people found some means or other of making a living, some returned to their former jobs, were absorbed largely in rural communities,[10] or made a living on black markets (marketers and brokers).

Second, the material losses as a result of the war accounted for 25 percent of national wealth, assets and structures, and 82 percent of ships. The reductions in light-industry capacity were conspicuous due to the wartime conversion to military production and equipment scraping.[11] (see Nakamura 1995, Tables 1.7 and 1.8, pp. 16–7.) Among others, energy and food were in grave shortage. Coal was the primary energy source in Japan—where production was at less than 40 percent of the wartime level. Starved for coal, even railway transport faced a crisis. Added to this was the grave shortage of food—where the rice crop was disastrously low at two-thirds the average annual crop in 1945 (Nakamura 1995, pp. 24, 35). The Japanese people were near starvation.

Third, rapid inflation developed. In addition to savings and public bonds that had been bought during the war, many military-related expenses (salaries, payments, compensation for loss, and so on.) flowed into circulation.[12]

3.4.1 Government Policy

To cope with the above hardships, the Japanese government took two important steps during the years 1946–1948.

First was to accelerate the recovery of productive capacity in major industries. The government directly oversaw the growth of coal and steel industries, which moved into operation in 1947. That is, the *priority production plan* (*Keisha seisan hoshiki*) where coal was put into the steel industry, then the produced steel into the coal industry. Reconstruction Bank[13] funds financed crude oil imports for injection into the coal and steel industries, which was important for the success of the system (Nakamura 1995, p. 35). The official prices of basic materials (such as steel, coal, fertilizer) were held below production costs, and the Reconstruction Bank provided subsidies to make up for the resulting deficits. Subsidized key industries included coal, fertilizers, electronic power, and iron and machinery. The government directly controlled prices and resource allocations.

The second step was to tame the three-digit inflation. The government invoked the Emergency Financial Measures Order in February 1946. This was a drastic action, "calling for the deposit of all cash in financial institutions, ordering the issue of new currency, implementing a 'new yen' conversion." The government "authorized each household to draw up to 500 yen per month in living expenses, and levying a property tax" (Nakamura 1995, p. 24) (100 billion yen according to the first draft, but finally amounting to about 30 billion yen). This was equivalent to the confiscation of assets through inflation.

By the order of the occupation authorities, the government suspended wartime indemnities, despite the government's public commitment to compensate business that had supported the war effort (July 1946).

The government adopted the Emergency Economic Measures in July 1947 that consisted of a wide-ranging comprehensive set of policies, which, in conjunction with the revival of production via the priority production system, was aimed at revising the official price structure and containing inflation. The official prices of basic material and wages were artificially held down and stabilized at a respective 65 times and 28 times their prewar levels. Inflation, however, continued unchecked. Wages increased due to wage hike movements, prices largely increased in the black market, and company deficits increased. By June 1948 the official price structure could no longer be maintained, and a revision had to be carried out. (see Nakamura

1995., pp. 36–7.) Despite these countermeasures, however, the government could not tame inflation.

3.4.2 The Dodge Plan

Despite every possible effort, the Japanese government could not combat inflation. The Supreme Commander for the Allied Powers (*SCAP*) appointed the American banker Joseph Dodge (chairman of the Detroit Bank) to work in Japan in 1948. He was credited with drafting West Germany's currency reform in 1945–1946. He visited Japan and guided a plan of fiscal and monetary policies to stop inflation. This was called Dodge plan.

The government put the Dodge plan in effect in 1949. His plan was to tighten and balance the fiscal budget, suspend new loans from the Reconstruction Bank, and reduce or abolish subsidies. The exchange rate was set at $1=360 yen. Lowering inflation brought Japan back to international trade. As a result, the economy went into a severe deflationary spiral, but severe recession was averted by the special export demand created by the Korean War (June 1950).[14] Japan was used as a supply base for the US and the United Nations troops. In fact, this became the springboard from which strong growth could begin.

With Japan's defeat at the end of world war II, it was expected, that the Japanese economy would face three serious problems: tremendous unemployment, near starvation, and rapid inflation. The government succeeded in the revival of production capacity in major industries and huge unemployment never materialized. However, the government was not able to curb inflation until the introduction of the Dodge Plan in 1949.

Notes

1. Japanese bureaucratic system: Japanese bureaucrats were considered to work efficiently. The Japanese bureaucratic system is "relatively independent of the executive heading cabinet, so that policy decisions are less politically motivated and more economy oriented." Furthermore, "career bureaucrats are expected to stay in the same ministry (with rotations) until their retirement; this ensures continuity and stability in strategic decision making" (Ito 1992, p. 203). In the next Chapter 4, Section 4.2, I will explain their policy decisions from these aspects.
2. Cominform is an abbreviation for the former USSR's Communist Information Bureau, and a successor to the Comintern. It was established upon Stalin's orders at a meeting in Poland (September 1947), its purpose being the coordination of the "voice" and activities of the communist parties of nine countries including the USSR. Cominform reflected a new hard line, expressing hostility toward the capitalist camp of the world, and was used by Stalin as an instrument for Soviet domination of Eastern Europe. After the rapprochement of the USSR and Yugoslavia in 1956, the Cominform was dissolved (Crystal (ed.) 2004).
3. The *zaibatsu* was controlled by the family-owned holding companies. Four zaibatsus (Mitsui, Mitsubishi, Sumiotomo, and Yasuda) were the largest. The zaibatsu was different from the popular *keiretsu* in Japan. The keiretsu consists of groups of affiliated companies, among which we observe various business group types. They are established around city banks, general trading companies or large industrial corporations, and they cross-share holdings

(through which group companies cement the relationship, and the parent company supports or influences affiliated companies).

4. Trust is a very large amalgamation of firms in the same industry to exclude or restrict competition. Cartel is an association of producers to regulate prices by restricting output and competition. Cartels are in principle illegal in many countries. A holding company is a company that controls another company or companies. Ownership may be complete or partial (ownership exceeding 51 percent of the voting right in the company). After the revision of the law in 1999, establishing a holding company became possible in Japan.

5. After World War II, two ideologically different blocks, one headed by the United States and the other by the USSR (Union of Soviet Socialist Republics), began to fiercely confront each other. These two blocks used diplomatic, economic, military, psychological, and other means to confront each other, as they would not bring on a full-scale war. This so-called Cold War ended with the collapse of the Berlin Wall in 1989.

6. During the red purge communist party members and their sympathizers were fired from private enterprises and public services.

7. (1) Lifetime employment is that regular employees in Japan are recruited right after their graduation from junior and senior high schools, junior college, or university and are expected to remain with the same employer for the rest of their careers. (2) The seniority wage system means that the wage increase depends on length of service to the company rather than an individual merit. (3) An enterprise union is a union that is organized on the basis of the enterprise or a workplace rather than a trade or an industry. The union includes all regular employees, both blue- and white-collar workers. See Nomura 2007 for the comprehensive study of the Japanese style of labor-management relationship.

8. There are currently 480 seats in the House of Representatives, among which single-seat constituency elects 300 and proportional representation constituency in regional blocs elects the remaining 180 seats. For the House of Councillors, there are currently 242 seats, in which half the seats are elected every 3 years by two ways: through electoral districts corresponding to prefectures and through one national district by proportional representation.

9. Rent seeking movement is activities which do not increase efficiency or production but result in a special position or monopoly power, and thus raise income.

10. Nakamura and Arai estimated that the rural communities absorbed a labor force of 18 million, about 4 million more than before the war (Nakamura 1995, Table 1.6, p. 15).

11. Some examples were rayon (15.5), staple fibers (22.6), cotton looms (28.9), and rayon looms (39.4). In the parentheses is the percent of production plant capacity at the end of war versus maximum wartime production capacity.

12. Nakamura (1995) mentions inflation in those years: "The consumer price index (including the black market) soared about 40 percent every 3 months in 1947, and even heading into 1948 it still continued to rise at a stiff 15 percent quarterly" (p. 35).

13. The Reconstruction Bank, established in January 1947, obtained its funds by issuing bonds accepted by the Bank of Japan. The bank made loans to public corporations and used the proceeds to subsidize key industries. Ito (1992, p. 58) mentions that the bank "became the primary machine for fiscal stimulation."

14. This special procurement was called *tokuju*, which consisted of the expenditures of the US Army and military personnel (Nakamura 1995, p. 45).

Chapter 4
Rapid Economic Growth

Why was Japan able to sustain rapid economic growth for nearly 20 years? There is no single reason. Various factors, ranging from general background to economic policies, have been analyzed. This chapter deals with Japan's general background, government policies, and some reasons for the rapid economic growth. For the government policy, we examine macroeconomic planning of the Economic Planning Agency (*EPA*), the industrial policy carried by the Ministry of International Trade and Industry (*MITI*), and last, foreign economic policy.

4.1 Some Outstanding Facts

Let us first observe some interesting facts during the period 1955–1973. Figure 4.1 shows the annual growth rate of Gross Domestic Fixed Capital Formation (*GDFCF*) by sector and Gross National Expenditure (*GNE*), and Fiscal Investment and Loans (*FIL*)-*GNE* ratio. We observe very high growth rates of *GDFCF*, particularly for private sectors, and a strong increasing trend of *FIL-GNE* ratio.

Table 4.1 shows these numerical values and some other related numbers. We can confirm high annual growth rates of Gross Fixed Capital Formation (*GFCF*) in private sectors, and also in the public sector. The growth rate in the public sector was relatively high during economic downturns, which to some extent made up for the low growth rate in the private sector. We also confirm a greater annual growth of the *FIL* (*Zaisei Toyushi*) program by the government, the meaning of which will be explained in the later section (see Section 4.3 for the *FIL*).

4.2 General Background

What was the general background or source of Japan's rapid economic growth? We will attempt to explain this economic growth by discussing Japan's political, international, and domestic business backgrounds. Let us begin with Japan's political background.

M. Iyoda, *Postwar Japanese Economy*, DOI 10.1007/978-1-4419-6332-1_4,
© Springer Science+Business Media, LLC 2010

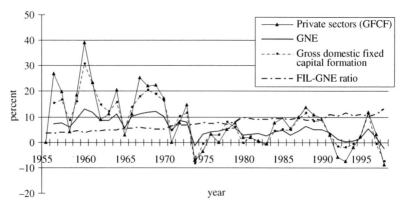

Fig. 4.1 Growth rate (private sectors (*GFCF*), *GDFCF* and *GNE*), and *FIL-GNE* Ratio.
Sources: Japan Statistical Association 2006, Vol. 1, 3–1, 5-10-a (data based on 1968 *SNA*)
Note: *GFCF* = Gross Fixed Capital Formation; *GDFCF* = Gross Domestic Fixed Capital Formation; *GNE* = Gross National Expenditure (at constant prices in calendar year 1990); *FIL-GNE* ratio = Fiscal Investment and Loans (fiscal year)/*GNE* (calendar year) (both at current prices)

4.2.1 Political Background

The San Francisco Peace Treaty restored Japan's sovereignty on April 28, 1952. The occupation of Japan by the Allied Powers ended. The Japanese–American Security Pact also concluded in 1952. From this date, Japan really became independent and was able to determine economic policies by itself.

The Japanese bureaucrats (particularly central government careers centered in Kasumigaseki, Tokyo) had the real power in the policy decisions through legislation. They supported the conservative party, and their ideology was economy-oriented; that is, they wanted Japan to be a great economic power. A fairly large number of the conservative party in the Diet were retired bureaucrats (see Sangyo Gakkai 1995, pp. 14–20).

In 1955, the *LDP* (Liberal Democratic Party) was formed by the merger of two major conservative parties (the Liberal Party and the Democratic Party), and the *SDP* (Social Democratic Party) was unified in the same year. The *LDP* held power until 1993 with the *SDP* as the main opposition. The split of the *LDP* after the general election precipitated a reorganization of the political party, including the founding of the *DPJ* (Democratic Party of Japan) in 1996. This was called "Parties system since 1955."[1] Although there were political disputes, political stability was maintained under this system, which provided the strong political base on which the Japanese society and economy developed.

During the eras of rapid growth cabinets were headed by Shigeru Yoshida (1948–1954) at first and lastly by Kakuei Tanaka (1972–1974). All were conservative cabinets in which the policy nuances were different as top priority was given to

Table 4.1 Annual growth rate of *GDFCF* and *FIL* and the percentage distribution in *GNE*

| | | Annual average growth rate | | | | | | Percentage distribution in GNE | | |
| | | GDFCF of which (sectors) | | | | | GDFCF | of which (sectors) | | |
Year	GNE	Private	Public	FIL		Year		Private	Public	FIL-GNE ratio
1956–60	8.7	21.7	10.7	16.2		1955	13.9	7.8	5.3	3.6
1961–65	9.2	13.3	16.3	23.4		1960	20.5	13.4	5.7	3.9
1966–70	11.1	19.7	12.5	16.5		1965	24.7	16.0	7.8	5.4
1971–73	7.0	7.3	13.3	25.1		1970	33.6	23.0	8.2	5.2
						1973	33.9	23.1	9.7	6.6

Note: Unit is %
Source: See Fig. 4.1

economic growth rather than stability. These cabinets took a policy to protect the capitalistic economic system and, among others, the most activist road to growth was during the administrations of Hayato Ikeda and then Kakuei Tanaka. Hayato Ikeda took office as prime minister in July 1960, and adopted his goal of "doubling income in 10 years"[2] in December 1960. The plan's aim was to attain full employment and higher living standards by pushing forward rapid economic growth at the rate of 7.2 percent. An average annual growth rate for 1959–1960 versus the previous year was 8.7 percent. Prime Minister Ikeda recognized the vigor of the Japanese economy. He declared his utmost confidence in the economy, which gave further confidence to the industrial leaders. Investment in private sectors greatly increased (see Fig. 4.1). The public was skeptical as to the success of the plan, but it was achieved in 7 years. The high rate of economic growth continued until the early 1970s.

Prime Minister Tanaka's cabinet took office in 1972. He "was still pursuing Ikeda's dream when he published his grandiose *Building a New Japan: A plan for Remodeling the Japanese Archipelago*, in which he quixotically ignored the fact of Japan's straightened circumstances in the changing times" (Nakamura 1995, p. 88; see Tanaka 1972). In the backdrop of high inflation, the oil crisis hit the world in 1973 and further accelerated the extremely high rate of inflation. Rapid economic growth in Japan came to an end.

4.2.2 International Background

After World War II, the worldwide economic growth rate was higher than that of the prewar years. The establishment of the International Monetary Fund (*IMF*, following the Breton Woods Conference, 1947) provided infrastructure support for world progress, by promoting increased international trade and balance-of-payments equilibrium. The General Agreement of Tariffs and Trade (*GATT*) is an international organization established in 1948 to promote the expansion of international trade through the removal of tariffs and other restrictions on cross-frontier trade. The *GATT* initiatives, together with the work of the *IMF*, and the formation of free trade blocks and high growth rates in industrial countries led to a record expansion of world trade up to the 1970s.[3] The prices of the raw materials and agricultural commodities, which Japan had no choice but to import, were relatively low.

4.2.3 Domestic Business Background

The *GHQ* imposed three major reforms (the antimonopoly measures, land reforms, and labor reforms), that made the Japanese economy more competitive and dynamic. After the zaibatsu dissolution and the purge of major companies' top management, the separation of ownership and management developed, and new managers appeared who were responsible for reconstruction and recovery. Fierce competition developed among the firms, which was supported by the stability of labor–management relations. Japanese-style labor relations established the lifetime employment system, the seniority wage system, and enterprise unions.

As we explained previously, there was a fitting background for the rapid economic growth. Political stability was maintained under the "Parties system since 1955." During the rapid economic growth period, the administration was conservative (the Liberal Democratic Party since 1955), which protected the capitalistic economic system. Internationally, *IMF* provided infrastructure support for the world progress and *GATT* promoted the expansion of international trade. Domestically, three reforms imposed by the *GHQ* brought in new managers and a competitive and dynamic economy.

4.3 Some Reasons for the Rapid Economic Growth

In this section, we present some reasons for Japan's rapid economic growth, with an emphasis on technological progress, high savings rate, and the budget of defense forces.

The first factor was the wide and huge technology improvement. In the early 1950 s, imports of foreign technology began, bringing a high rate of continuous production increases. Nakamura (1995, pp. 76–77 and 82) points out the following: (1) "Japan's ability to assimilate this technology was to a great extent shaped by prewar and wartime technological experience." (2) The order in which the technology developed, "beginning with the materials and basic industries such as steel and electric power, then shifting to electric machinery, and finally proceeding to the new assembly industries like automobiles and electronics." (3) Japan produced very little technology of its own in the 1950 s and 1960 s; however, Japan's achievement "was the combining of numerous imported technologies to create low-cost mass production systems."[4]

The second factor was the high savings rate of Japan, which provided sufficient funds to support the high investment rate. What produced this high rate of savings? After examining the literature regarding this question, Nakamura (1995, pp. 102–104) considers the following two factors as the most powerful in explaining Japan's high rate of savings: "(1) Increases in real income which accompanied Japan's high rate of growth. (2) Increases in the proportion of bonuses and other temporary income."

For the policy side, the Japanese tax and financial systems played important roles in the high savings rate and this came under the oversight of the Ministry of Finance (hereafter *MoF*). Various kinds of preferential taxes on income from assets that were implemented in Japan under the Shoup tax reform contributed to this high rate of savings (as mentioned in Chapter 3). As a result, the Japanese effective rate of progressive tax was largely decreased.[5] A strong financial system funneled money from domestic savers to domestic investors. The funds were then invested in railways, roads, schools, hospitals, housing, and soon. For this, the Japanese government made the best use of the *FIL* program (what we call *Zaisei Toyushi*[6]), which largely depended on the Postal Savings System.

Third, the budgets for defense forces were very low, and funds were directed to improve social infrastructures and government investment projects.[7] The Japanese military spending was small scale relative to that of other countries. It has been held down to less than one percent of *GNP*(now, *GNI*).

Fourth, Japan's monetary and fiscal authorities made sound policy decisions during the period 1955–1964. The government was prohibited by law from issuing deficit bonds (bonds to finance the general budget) until 1965. Even after the law was changed, the government deficit did not become large until 1975. Balancing the budget was essential to rapid growth to avoid the crowding-out effect.[8] (see Ito 1992, p. 64, Ikeda (ed.) 2008, pp. 321–322).

We note some reasons for the rapid economic growth. However, an introduction of foreign technology and the high savings rate and its use were closely related to economic policy: low budgets for defense forces and balancing the government budgets (sound policy) were *per se* policy.

4.4 Government Policy

The government concentrated on promoting investment and exports. We have already mentioned some of the government policies (tax system and *zaisei toyushi,* and so on) in the previous section. In this section, we discuss macroeconomic planning, industrial policy, and foreign economic policy.

4.4.1 Macroeconomic Planning

The Economic Planning Agency (hereafter *EPA*, which was integrated into the Cabinet Office in 2001) was charged with macroeconomic planning. Since 1955, *EPA* has announced 5-year plans, setting targets for the growth rate of *GNP* and its demand components. The plans were *indicative and more forecast-oriented* than directives. The proposed plans signaled the government's commitment to growth, giving confidence to industrial leaders. As a result, actual growth outpaced each of EPA's plans until the first oil crisis. Most of the plans were 5–6 years, but the average life span until the 13th plan was about 3.2 years.

Table 4.2 shows the Japanese economic plans. As Nakamura (1995, pp. 91 and 94–5) mentions, the plans possess three basic characteristics. They indicate (1) the desired direction of economic and social development; (2) the policy direction that the government should take to achieve these ends; and (3) behavior guidelines for the people and businesses.

In this table, we observe four periods. The first (1–3) was the period that the achievement of economic independence and full employment were the leading issues. The second (4–7) was the period in which distortions of the rapid economic growth—for example, pollutions, inflation under the low unemployment rate, and over- and de-populated areas—were dealt with. The third (8–12) was the period in which the government, more than its preceding plans, shifted from rapid growth

Table 4.2 Government economic plans

Name of plan	Adapted date (Cabinet)	Plan period (years)	Objectives	Growth rate (%) Planned: (achieved)
(1) Five-year economic self-support plan	December 1955 (Hatoyama)	FY1956–1960 (5 years)	Economic independence; full employment	4.9(8.8)
(2) New long-range economic plan	December 1957 (Kishi)	FY1958–1962 (5 years)	Maximum growth; higher living standard; full employment	6.5(9.7)
(3) National income doubling plan	December 1960 (Ikeda)	FY1961–1970 (10 years)	Maximum stable growth for full employment and higher living standards	7.8(10.0)
(4) Medium-term economic plan	January 1965 (Sato)	FY1964–1968 (5 years)	Correction of distortions	8.1(10.1)
(5) Economic and social development plan	March 1967 (Sato)	FY1967–1971 (5 years)	Development for a balanced and rich economy and society	8.2(9.8)
(6) New economic and social development plan	May 1970 (Sato)	FY1970–1975 (6 years)	Building a livable Japan through balanced economic development	10.6(5.1)
(7) Basic economic and social development plan	February 1973 (Tanaka)	FY1973–1977 (5 years)	Simultaneous achievement of improved national welfare and promotion of international cooperation	9.4(3.5)
(8) Economic plan for the latter half of the 1970s	May 1976 (Miki)	FY1976–1980 (5 years)	Extrication from recession and movement toward new growth path; countermeasures to reduced growth rate	6.0(4.5)

Table 4.2 (Continued)

Name of plan	Adapted date (Cabinet)	Plan period (years)	Objectives	Growth rate (%) Planned: (achieved)
(9) Seven-year plan for the new economic society	August 1979 (Ohira)	FY1979–1985 (7 years)	Movement toward a stable growth path; improvement in the national welfare; effort to develop the international economy	5.7(3.9)
(10) Outlook and guidelines for the economic society of the 1980s	August 1983 (Nakasone)	FY1983–1990 (8 years)	Establishment of stable international relations; formation of a vital economic society; securing a rich national life	4.0(4.5)
(11) Five-year plan for the economic management of Japan	May 1988 (Takeshita)	FY1988–1992 (5 years)	Correction of trade imbalance; improving people's quality of life; developing the regionally balanced economic society	3.75(4.0)
(12) Five-year plan for a quality-of-life-superpower	June 1992 (Miyazawa)	FY1992–1996 (5 years)	Achieving quality of life; harmony with rest of the world; and stable international development	3.5(1.9)

Table 4.2 Government economic plans

Name of plan	Adapted date (Cabinet)	Plan period (years)	Objectives	Growth rate (%) Planned: (achieved)
(13) Economic and social plan for the structural change	January 1995 (Murayama)	FY1995–2000 (6 years)	Creation of the free and vital economic society; creation of the affluent and safe society; participation in the global society	3.0(1.2)
(14) Appropriate image of the economic society and the policy line of economic rebirth	July 1999 (Obuchi)	FY1999–2008 (about 10 years)	Formation of the diverse wisdom society; preparation for the declining birthrate and aging population; adaptation of the globalization; environments and harmony	2.0(0.7)

Notes: (1) Achieved growth rates are based on the new *SNA* database (base year = 1990); for plans 13 and 14 based on 93*SNA* (base year = 2000); (2) English expression from (1) to (12) followed Nakamura's Table 3.9 (pp. 92–93); (3) The planned growth rate in real terms in plan 8 is a little over than the proposed level, and, since plan 9, shows an approximate level
Source: ESRI of CAO (b) (2004), Transitions of Long-Term Government Economic Plans

to those goals seeking harmony with the rest of the world and improving the Japanese people's quality of life. The fourth (13–14) may be the period of reactivating the economy under the new line of economic rebirth, which deals with the wisdom society, the declining birthrate, the aging population, globalization, and environment.

4.4.2 Industrial Policy

The Ministry of International Trade and Industry (hereafter *MITI*, which was later renamed the Ministry of Economy, Trade and Industry) was charged with industrial policy. *MITI* wisely guided investment by setting target to identify sunrise industries and nursing them to production quickly. Targeted industries were steel, shipbuilding, chemicals, and so on. *MITI* used two tools for nursing them. First was the allocation of foreign reserves for the purchase of capital equipment and raw materials. Second was the subsidization of loans for investment in structures and equipment through government financial agencies such as the Japan Development Bank.[9] These processes brought great technological progress and increased aggregate demand.

MITI also guided the industry in averting excessive competition due to overcapacity. As private domestic funds became abundant and trade surplus swelled foreign reserves in the 1960s, *MITI* changed its policies. It supplied administrative guidance (*gyosei shidou*[10]) to regulate the speed of investment, averting excessive competition due to overcapacity. The investment plans of firms were coordinated, falling within *MITI*'s projections of demand expansion.

Some of Japan's star industries (consumer electronics and precision optical products) however were not targeted. An interesting fact was that the automobile companies opposed and stopped *MITI*'s plan to exploit economies of scale in 1955, and refused to follow *MITI*'s encouragement to merger firms to attain economies of scale in order to compete with foreign producers in the early 1960 s (Hsu 1999, p. 227; Ito 1992, p. 202).[11]

As the rapid economic growth continued, the Japanese labor market became tight, particularly in the early 1960s. The unemployment rate was between 1.4 percent and 1.1 percent during the period 1961–1974. The labor shortage was primarily met with people from farming areas (see Chapter 2, Figs. 2.6a,b). Therefore, industry adjustment was smooth on a macro level, although people working in the declining industries such as coal and textiles had to move for getting jobs.

4.4.3 Foreign Economic Policy

Japan followed a free trade policy, but with such exceptions as the capital control against foreign capital and the infant industry protection.[12] The fixed exchange rate continued, making the costs of production cheaper as the relative productivity to other countries increased.

Japan became a member nation of *OECD* in 1964, the same year it hosted the Olympics and decided to liberalize capital transactions. However, it was in December 1980 that capital transactions became free in principle. Reflecting the increase in trade surplus since 1981, Japanese capital exports have increased greatly. As a result, Japanese net foreign assets led the world in size in 1985. Since then, Japan has maintained this top position in most years. On the other hand, however, capital imports from overseas were extremely low. The capital import/export ratio was very low. Since 1999, the ratio has greatly increased; however, the average ratio was still 22 percent in 1999–2008. (see Fig. 2.8 in Chapter 2.)

The fixed exchange rate continued until Nixon Shock or dollar shock (1971). Since 1958, the overall US international balance of payments has become negative; however, trade surplus more or less covered capital deficit and overseas military and economic aids. Reflecting the weakening international competitiveness of its industries, the United States experienced its first trade deficit in 1971. Gold reserves declined to a critical level of nearly 10 billion dollars. Then President Nixonsuspended the convertibility of the dollar into gold—the gold and dollar standard on August 15, 1971—creating a great blow to the world economy. As a result, the fixed exchange rate system moved in the float. The Japanese yen revalued upward by 17 percent in January 1972 (Jiyu Kokumin-sha 1976, pp. 433–434).

Various factors mentioned above contributed to Japan's rapid economic growth. Singling any factor out is difficult; however, the entrepreneurial spirit, among others, might be the most important driving force for the rapid economic growth. This was the so-called animal spirits that John Maynard Keynes (1936, p. 161) raised, and was later stressed by Joan Robinson (1960, p. 146). From this viewpoint, the following two factors are also important. First,, the introduction of the purge of major companies' top management new managers after the zaibatsu dissolution carried on the spirit of economic growth. Second, in the background was the strong government policy that contributed to promoting investment and exports.

Notes

1. During the period of "Parties system since 1955," we observed both rapid economic growth and moderate economic growth. Exceptions were the periods strongly affected by the first oil crisis and the collar bubble economy.
2. Osamu Shimomura, a Ministry of Finance bureaucrat, recognizing Japan's high growth potential, was key in promoting the plan, which called for improvement of infrastructures, advanced economic structure, promotion of trade and international cooperation, development of human capital and science technology, easing dual structures, and achievement of social stability. As a result, the plan was accomplished in 7 years, but caused negative effects such as social imbalance between private and public investment, a high rate of inflation, and environmental disruption. Some interesting points are an introduction of the improvement of infrastructures (planned on a 1/2 ratio of public investment (infrastructures) to private investment; and the fact that the plan reduced difference problems (such as income and productivity) by the size of the company and regional location.

3. The World Trade Organization (*WTO*) was established in 1995 to replace *GATT* as the international framework for international trade negotiations. As a result, *GATT* was abolished in 1995.

4. During World War II, a great deal of technology was developed in Japan for military purposes. After the war, a range of technology over a much broader spectrum was developed and its individual applications were pursued.

5. Quoting Morita (1961), Nakamura shows the estimated effective tax rate (expressed by percentages of gross income) of 4.4 percent to 34.3 percent among ten major industries; however, an average rate of eight industries excluding lowest two industries was 30.9 percent (see Table 2.9 utilization of the special tax measures by major corporations, Nakamura 1995, p. 49).

6. *Zaisei Toyushi,* a system planned by the government (*MoF*), did not use taxes but savings for public corporations and government financial institutions. Postal savings, publicly saved savings, pension funds, and so on were used. In Fig. 4.1 we observe a strong increasing trend of *FIL-GNE* ratio. However, the system became so bloated that it often supported inefficient investment and encroached upon the private sector. Koizumi's government made a sweeping reform of this system in 2001. The government abolished the Trust Fund Bureau of the Ministry of Finance and the number of funded institutions and corporations was reduced. The Postal Saving System was privatized in 2007.

7. This reflected the Japanese elder statesman Yoshida's view that "armaments should be curbed and military spending suppressed while all efforts were concentrated on the reconstruction of the economy" (Nakamura 1995, p. 88).

8. Crowding-out is the process where an increase in government borrowing displaces private spending. If an increase in government borrowing has a large effect on interest rates, private spending will fall as investors slim down their plans.

9. The Japan Development Bank was established in 1951 for the economic reconstruction and the promotion of the development of industries, which succeeded the loan assets of the Reconstruction Bank and the collateral funds of the US economic aid to Japan.

10. *Gyosei shido* refers to the suggestions or "unwritten orders" given by Japanese bureaucrats to firms in order to implement official policies. All government ministries and agencies practice this in their interactions with the private sector; among others, *MITI* and *MoF* were particularly active in its use.

11. With the foreign exchange allocation system, extreme restrictions were imposed on automobile imports until the early 1960s. Therefore, the automobile industry was assured of a domestic market for its development (Nakamura 1995, p. 48).

12. Infant industries (newly established industries) are a legitimate area for the application of protectionism. They are often subsidized by the government and/or protected from imports in the hope that they can exploit economies of scale and thus eventually withstand foreign competition.

Chapter 5
Results of the Rapid Economic Growth: Positive Effects

This chapter deals with the positive results of the rapid economic growth describing each of these in detail. Economic growth is generally measured by the growth rate of *GDP* (previously *GNP*).

5.1 General Economic Results

What did the economic growth bring us? What were its results? The obvious economic results were greater increases in real *GDP*, per capita *GDP*, and real wages, to which the high productivity growth rate largely contributed. The rapid economic growth contributed to high income and the low unemployment rate, but at the same time, it caused high consumer price increases in Japan.

Table 5.1 shows some results of economic growth during the period 1955–1973. *GDP* (real) increased by a factor of 4.3 (annual average growth rate, 9.3 percent). Per capita *GDP* (real) naturally increased by a factor of 3.6 (7.3 percent). Real wages increased by a factor of 3.4 (7.3 percent).

We observe many areas of improvement that reflected the income growth, including the growth rate of durable consumer goods, the number of persons and the levels assisted by the livelihood protection, medical care insurance, and pension. Infrastructures were dual. Some infrastructures, such as schools, hospitals, water supply, national roads, and so on improved during the rapid economic growth period. As a whole, however, infrastructures lagged behind production capital causing social imbalance. We examine this distortion in the next chapter. We briefly deal with the improvement in income distribution.

5.2 Spreading Rate of Durable Consumer Goods, and Others

5.2.1 Spreading Rate of Durable Consumer Goods

Figure 5.1 shows the increasing rate of durable consumer goods of Japan. As a result of income growth, people could afford new durable consumer goods, which made the standard of living better and more convenient. Many of these new goods

M. Iyoda, *Postwar Japanese Economy*, DOI 10.1007/978-1-4419-6332-1_5,
© Springer Science+Business Media, LLC 2010

Table 5.1 Some results of the rapid economic growth (1955–1973)

	1955	1973	Increase ratio of 1973–1955	Annual growth rate (%)
GDP (real)	52,271.0	225,120.8	4.3	9.25
GNP (real)	52,460.9	225,170.2	4.3	9.23
Per capita GDP				
(real)	580.3	2,063.4	3.6	7.3
(nominal)	94($261)	1,035($3,360)		
Real wages (employees)	1,056.4	3,545.2	3.4	7.3
Per capita wages (employees) (nominal)	194.4($540)	1528.0($4,961)		
Labor productivity			3.3	7.0
of which manufacturing			4.6	8.9
Unemployment rate (%)	2.5	1.3		1.52 (average of 1955–1973)

Notes: Real values are at market prices in calendar year 1990. Real wages are deflated by *CPI* index (1990=100). *GDP* (real) and *GNP* (real) are in billions of yen, and others are in thousands of yen

Sources: Japan Statistical Association (2006), Vol. 1, 3-3-a, 3-4, 3-6 and key statistics, p. 84; Vol. 4, 19–4 and 19–8-a. SB of MCA (a) (1991), p. 44; (1987), p. 46

including washers, refrigerators, and black and white TVs, were considered status symbols in the 1960s. These status symbols were called holy durables and were compared to the three symbols (sword, mirror, and comma-shaped bead) of the Emperor when he ascends the throne.

We observe the very steep rate of increased durable consumer goods spending. Furthermore, in the 1970s, the Japanese people adopted three new status symbols, cars, air conditioning, and color TV sets. Perhaps the class consciousness Japanese set these symbols as living standards because according to a government opinion poll, about 90 percent of the respondents identified at the end of the rapid growth period said that they belonged to the middle class.

5.2.2 Class Consciousness

Table 5.2 shows that, during the period 1958–1973, the middle class greatly increased to 90.2 percent from 72.4 percent and the lower class declined to 5.5 percent from 17.0. Among the middle class, the "middle" increased to 61.3 percent from 37.0 and the "low" declined to 22.1 percent from 32.0. Since 1973, the total middle class percentage has kept to that high level until recently, varying from 87.3 to 91.4. CAO of GoJ (2007, p. 330) compares similar surveys regarding the awareness of social stratification, and concludes that there is not a very large difference in middle class identification among Japan, the United States, and Germany.

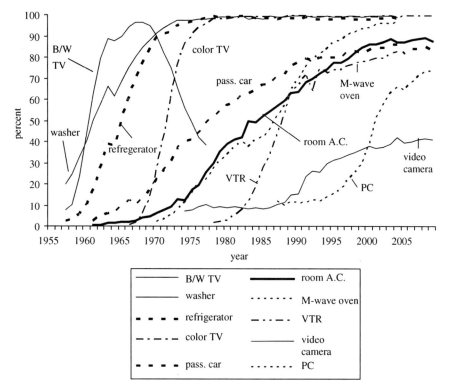

Fig. 5.1 Spreading rate of durable consumer goods.
Sources: ESRI, CAO (b) (2004), (8) (pp. 24–27); (2009), (12) (pp. 30–31). IB of EPA (b) (1963, 1970, and 1977)

Table 5.2   Class consciousnesses of the Japanese (%)

Year	High	Middle	Of which upper	middle	low	Low
1958	0.2	72.4	3.4	37.0	32.0	17.0
1965	0.4	86.0	7.0	50.0	29.0	8.0
1973	0.6	90.2	6.8	61.3	22.1	5.5
1990	0.7	89.0	8.2	53.1	27.7	7.2
2005	1.1	91.4	11.0	54.1	26.3	6.0

Source: GIOMS of CAO (2006), extracted from Figs: 45

5.2.3 Engel Coefficient

The Engel coefficient is defined as "food expenditure/living expenditure." This coefficient is generally used to measure living standards. Table 11.2 in Chapter 11 shows this coefficient, which declined to 22.7 percent in 2005 from 38.7 percent in 1963.

Nowadays, Japanese households (with two or more members) spend less than a quarter of their living expenditure on food.

Engel's law of economics states that with given tastes or preferences, the proportion of income spent on food diminishes as incomes increase. German social statistician Ernest Engel (1821–1896) developed this formula in a paper published in 1857 by examining the ratio of the consumption by group of items to the living expense of Belgian workers' households.

5.3 Social Security

5.3.1 Livelihood Protection

Table 5.3 shows the number of persons and the level that are assisted by livelihood protection. We observe that average amount assisted per person expressed by "amount assisted per person/per capita income of worker's households (in Tokyo Metropolis) was 39.1 percent in 1955.

Table 5.3 Livelihood protection, health insurance, and pension

Fiscal year	Average amount assisted per person[a] (%)	Assisted numbers (per 1,000 persons)	Persons assisted (in 10,000)	Coverage of health insurance (%)	Pension benefits ratio to annual income[b] (%)	Insurance rate[c] (pension) (%)
1955	39.1	21.6	193	68.6		
1960	38.0	17.4	163	94.7	(1961) 25.1	(1961) 3.5
1965	50.2	16.3	160	98.2		
1970	54.1	13.0	134	99.3		
1975	60.9	12.1	135	99.4	(1973) 61.8	(1973) 7.6
1980		12.2	143			
1985		11.8	143			
1990		8.2	101			
1995		7.0	88			
2000		8.4	107			
2005		11.6	147		(2003) 63.6	(2003) 13.58

[a]Amount assisted per person/per capita income of workers' households (Tokyo Metropolis)
[b]Model pension benefit for a couple/average male income by remuneration class (employees)
[c]Split half between labor and management
Sources: Takayama (1980), Table 5.1, Japan Statistical Association (2006), Vol. 5, 23–37, and MHLW (2008), resources. IB of EPA (a) (1963, p. 265; 1984, p. 297). Nihon Keizai Shinbun (Japanese Economic Newspaper) (November 28, 2003) based on the sources of MHLW and the Pension Fund Association

Reflecting economic growth, the ratio increased to 60.9 percent in 1975. Since then, this level has been more or less maintained. Numbers (of assisted person) per 1,000 persons were 21.6 (which was equivalent to 2.16 percent of total population) in 1955, declined significantly to 7.0 in 1995, and then, reflecting economic stagnation, the number again increased. We can also confirm these phenomena as shown by the number of persons assisted in the middle column in Table 5.3, which was 1.93 million (1955). This number also significantly declined to 0.88 million in 1995, and then again increased.[1]

There has been an argument about the latent number of persons who need assistance. Along the poverty line level, the number of the assisted persons should be far greater. However, people below the poverty line have not always claimed livelihood protection from the government.[2] It seems, until recently, that a large number of Japanese have not considered that they were entitled to government assistance. (see Chapter 6, Section 6.4.2 for a further argument about the real reason.)

5.3.2 Health Insurance and Pension

The National Health Insurance for the self-employed was established in 1961 setting up the universal medical care system in Japan. Health insurance already existed for employees of corporations and public services. As a result, coverage of medical insurance increased to more than 99 percent (1970) from 68.6 (1955). The Japanese state pension covering the self-employed also began in 1961, bringing a universal pension system to Japan. Until then, employees of corporations and public services each had their own pensions. In the initial stage, "benefits ratio to annual (male) income" was 25.1 percent. Reflecting economic growth, this percentage increased to 61.8 in 1973, and was maintained at essentially the same level until recently in 2003 (Table 5.3). The "benefit ratio of a joint life annuity to after-tax income of the standard family" was 59.3 percent in 2003 (see Chapter 11, Table 11.4 for the details).

5.4 Infrastructure (Social Overhead Capital)

Infrastructure (social overhead capital) is accumulated capital from investment, usually by the government or local authorities: examples include nation's roads, railways, ports, housing, hospitals, parks, schools, water supply, and so on. These are broadly classified into two types namely, industrial infrastructures and living infrastructures (public assets related to daily life).

Prime Minister Hayato Ikeda adapted a "National Income Doubling Plan" (1960), which was an epoch moment in Japan as it was the first time that the term infrastructure (or social overhead capital) was introduced into the policy terminology. The plan was based on the recognition that infrastructure (Kanamori et al. 1981, pp. 1097–98), particularly industrial infrastructure, lags behind the private production capital, which causes a bottleneck in economic growth. The industrial infrastructure should be improved to free up this bottleneck. Second, capital improvement is needed for public assets related to daily life to improve national living. Third, the improvement of infrastructure increases economic growth. Ikeda's plan called for infrastructure improvement by sector, which greatly contributed to the improved Japanese infrastructure.

Since Ikeda's plan, every economic plan has followed the same goal of setting
infrastructure improvement by sector. In this background, the ratio of gross fixed
capital formation of general government to *GDP* increased from 3.9 (1960), 4.5
(1970) to 6.1 percent (1980) (source: Japan Statistical Association 2006, Vol. 1,
3–1). Gross fixed capital formation of general government represents Japanese public investment. Figure 5.2 shows the percentage distribution of the Japanese social
overhead capital investment by major sector. The figure reflects economic plans,
and during the rapid economic growth period, we observe some characteristics of
the Japanese infrastructure investment. The first type shows that the greater amount
of investment was carried out in the early stage, but was gradually decreased: such
investments were in schools and social education, conservation of national land, and
railways. Another type was a growing investment such as in roads, sewerage and
water supply, rental houses, and telegraph and telephone. By rough classification,
aviation and harbor, and major parts of both road and railways are industry-related

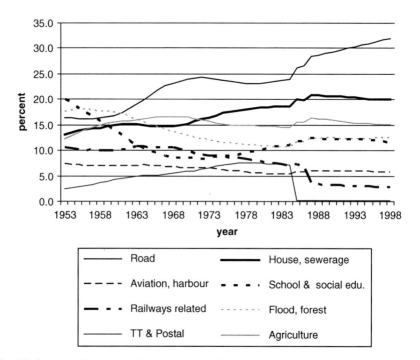

Fig. 5.2 Social overhead capital investment by major sector.
Source: Japan Statistical Association (2006), Vol. 2, 9–4 (total of 20 sectors at current prices)
Notes: (1) Major sectors in the figure are road, aviation (aviation, harbor, and industrial water
supply); TT & Postal (telegraph and telephone, postal service); railway related (national railway,
Japan railway construction, subways); house and sewerage (rental house, sewerage, waste, water
supply, park); school and social education; flood, forest (flood control, forest conservation, sea-
coast); agriculture (agriculture, forestry, fisheries, state-owned forest); (2) Irregular variations in
the mid-1980s reflect privatization of public corporations such as the Japan Telegraph & Telephone
and the Japan National Railroad

infrastructures; rental houses, sewerage and water supply, telegraph and telephone, and some parts of railway and road are considered infrastructures related to daily life.

5.5 Income Distribution

In Chapter 2 we observed a trend of Japanese income distribution and mentioned a strong equalizing trend in the 1960s. Figure 5.3 shows *CV* (coefficient of variance[3]) of per capita prefectural income and the Gini coefficient of income distribution. This Gini is a reproduction of Fig. 2.4, Gini (1) (workers' households with two persons or more, before tax). The *CV* of per capita prefecture income shows a declining trend in the 1960s, meaning an equalizing trend of local income. During the observation period of 1955–1974, the spread of the per capita income by prefecture was becoming smaller, though with fluctuations, which might correspond to the equalizing trend of income distribution of the entire economy. We understand that income distribution had a strong equalizing trend in both the national and the local economies in the 1960s.

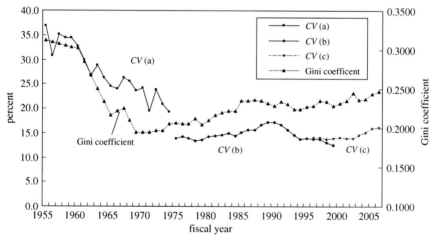

Fig. 5.3 Coefficient of valiance (*CV*) and Gini coefficient.
Sources: DNA (Department of National Accounts), ESRI (Economic and Social Research Institute), CAO (b), Data for 1955–1974 and 1975–1999 downloaded from (www.esri.cao.go.jp/jp/sna/kenmin/68sna_s30/main.html); *CV(c)* obtained from DNA of ESRI, CAO (b) (2009), Fig. 1; Gini coefficient obtained by simple calculation from CAO (2007), Sources 2, (2)
Notes: 1. (a) National income by prefecture based on 68*SNA* for 1955–1974 at 1980 market prices (CAO's estimates); (b) 68*SNA* for 1975–1999 at 1990 market prices (prefecture's own estimates); and (c) 93*SNA* for 1996–2004 at 2000 market prices. 2. *CV*(a), *CV*(b), and *CV*(c) are respectively calculated by (a), (b), and (c) above. The author calculates the first two. 3. Gini coefficient are workers' households (with two persons or more, before tax). The same as that in Fig. 2.4

We observed various positive effects of economic growth. An obvious result was outstanding income growth (*GDP*, per capita *GDP*, real wages) and the low unemployment rate. As a result, we saw the following positive effects:

First, we observed that the high growth spreading rate of durable consumer goods indicated that these goods were considered status symbols in the 1960s and 1970s. According to a class-consciousness survey, the middle class greatly increased and the lower class fairly decreased. Engel's coefficient also largely decreased. Second, there were various kinds of improvement in social security. The government introduced universal medical care and pension systems, and medical care insurance coverage and pension benefits ratio greatly increased. Livelihood protection greatly improved in terms of average amount assisted per person and the number of assisted persons greatly declined. Third, there was great improvement in infrastructures, which was due to "Economic Plans" that set the goal of infrastructure improvement by sector. Fourth, income distribution largely improved on both the national and the local levels in the 1960s.

Notes

1. Japanese household standard assisted by the livelihood protection (MHLW 2008): family composition (33 year old male, 29 year old female, and 4 year old child), and assisted amount (162,170 yen for the first class urban area in 2004–2008, meaning the highest amount in this category). For the aged couple (68-year-old male and 65-year-old female), the assisted amount was 121,940 yen under the same first class urban area in 2004–2008.
2. For example, OECD (2006, Table 4.12) sets the poverty line at the half level of median income in the country. According to this report, Japan ranked fifth at 15.3 percent in 2000 following behind Ireland. The poverty line is not the level of minimum entitlement for government support in Japan. See Chapter 10 for the discussion about the Japanese poverty rate.
3. The coefficient of variance is a technical expression explaining the dispersion of the variable. It is measured by standard deviation divided by mean. The larger the coefficient of variance, the greater the spread of the per capita income by prefecture. (Variance is a measure of the degree of dispersion in a series of numbers around their mean.).

Chapter 6
Results of the Rapid Economic Growth: Negative Effects or Distortions

Economic growth brought various kinds of positive results; however, it also brought some kinds of negative effects or distortions. In this chapter, we deal with social imbalance, overpopulation in metropolitan areas, environmental disruption, inflation, and low-income groups.

6.1 Social Imbalance

The expansion in infrastructure development became unbalanced. As many infrastructures rapidly improved during the rapid economic growth period, many fell behind production capital and public assets related to daily life (living infrastructures) lagged further behind industrial infrastructures, causing social imbalance. Galbraith (1998, p. 195) mentions, "The inherent tendency will always be for public services to fall behind private production."[1] This brought a serious social imbalance, in particular during the rapid economic growth period. Galbraith defines *social balance* as "a satisfactory relationship between the supply of privately produced goods and services and those of the state" (1998, p. 189).

Figure 6.1 shows that public investment fell behind private investment and the gap between these increased until the early 1970s.

Since Ikeda's plan (1960) every economic plan has followed the goal of setting the infrastructure improvement by sector. (see Chapter 5, Section 5.4.) During the rapid economic growth period, however, social imbalance became greater, causing social maladies such as pollution, congestion, and so on. The problems appeared particularly in metropolitan areas in the form of commuting, traffic congestion, housing problems, and so on. The problems discussed below were more or less the result. (In Fig. 6.1, we also observe that social imbalance grew after the second oil crisis lasting until the bubble burst.)

6.2 Concentration to Metropolitan Areas

Figure 6.2 shows the trend of population growth for various areas in 5-year periods since 1960. During the 1960–1965 period, the growth rate for both the metropolitan and Tokyo areas exceeded 15 percent, whereas, the greatly negative growth rate was

M. Iyoda, *Postwar Japanese Economy*, DOI 10.1007/978-1-4419-6332-1_6,
© Springer Science+Business Media, LLC 2010

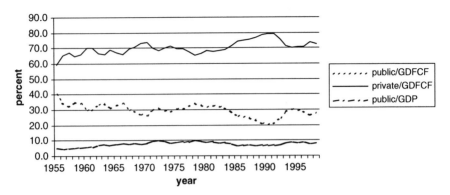

Fig. 6.1 Investment by sector.
Sources: Japan Statistical Association (2006), Vol. 1, 3–1 (calculated at constant prices, base year=1990)
Note: GDFCF (gross domestic fixed capital formation)

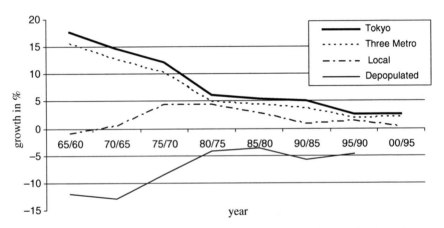

Fig. 6.2 The trend of population growth (Depopulated, three metropolitan and local areas).
Sources: Study Group on Activation Policy for the Depopulated Areas (1999), Fig. 2-2-2 (with extension by the current author)
Note: Three metropolitan areas—Tokyo area (Saitama, Chiba, Tokyo, and Kanagawa), Osaka area (Kyoto, Osaka, and Hyogo), and Nagoya area (Aichi); local areas (all others excluding three metropolitan areas), and depopulated areas (local cities, towns, and villages designated by law)

in depopulated areas. These trends continued to the 1970–1975 period, and then began to slow down.

During that period, the young generation moved out their hometowns, and aged people remained in depopulated areas. The farming lands gradually became wastelands and could no longer provide a living or jobs in those areas. The Japanese government took serious countermeasures in this area. The government put the Act on Special Measures for Depopulated Areas in effect for a limited time of 10 years (1970). The government planned to spend a huge amount of money (7.9 trillion yen = 21.9 billion dollars) on depopulated areas. In 1980, the government extended the act for another 10 years, and planned to spend 20 trillion yen (88.2 billion dollars).

The population outflow slowed down and there was considerable material improvement on the social overhead capital to roads, waterworks, schools, public halls, museums, parks, hospitals, and so on. However, the problem in these areas mentioned above remained. Improvements of the infrastructure are important for both living standards and the development of industry. They cannot tie local people to their areas unless they are successful in actually developing industry in those areas or providing business opportunities for these local people.

On the other hand, overpopulated areas also resulted in high living costs and housing problems (small but expensive spaces). Other problems included air and noise pollution, traffic jams, and increasing traffic accidents. Under such serious social imbalance, fundamental social justice and achieving the living standard improvements will not function properly. Restoring the social balance may be a question of adjustment between the private wants and public needs, which is at the same time a question of how economic growth is even distributed.

6.3 Environmental Disruption

Environmental disruption was one of the worst consequences of the rapid economic growth period. At that time it was said that the familiar abbreviation GNP could stand for "Gross National Pollution" (Tsuru 1993, p. 129).

6.3.1 General Background

The outstanding features of the environmental disruption process were as follows: First was an extremely rapid expansion of heavy and chemical industries that were generally more polluting than other industries. Second was the progress in the degree of urbanization far in excess of demographic changes (see the population growth by area in Fig. 6.2). Third was the explosive boom in the mass consumption market, notably private cars. All of these caused woeful lags in the provision of complementary social overhead capital (port facilities, sewerage system, roads, and so on). (see Tsuru 1993, p. 131.)

Table 6.1 shows the environmental disruption. The numbers of injury as a result of pollution greatly increased from 20,502 (1966) to 87,764 (1972, the peak until 2000), declining in the mid-1990s, and then again increasing to 100,323 (2003, the peak). Among the typical seven injury, the biggest number is attributed to air pollution, the second from noise problems, and the third is smell. Waste products are currently the biggest number in the category of "others."

Table 6.1   Environmental disruption (Claim numbers to pollution)

Fiscal year	Total[a]		Typical 7[b] among which air pollution	water contamination	noises, vibration	smell	Others among which waste products
1966	20,502	19,517	4,962	2,197	8,833	3,494	985
1968	28,970	27,398	5,843	3,782	12,110	5,622	1,572
1970	63,433	59,467	12,911	8,913	22,568	14,997	3,986
1972	87,764	79,727	15,096	14,197	28,632	21,576	8,037
1975	76,531	67,315	11,873	13,453	23,812	17,516	9,216
1980	64,690	54,809	9,282	8,269	24,094	12,900	9,881
1985	64,550	51,413	9,036	7,617	21,946	12,553	13,137
1990	74,294	49,359	9,496	7,739	20,431	11,423	24,935	5,029
1995	61,364	42,701	10,013	6,763	15,552	10,131	18,663	4,065
2000	83,381	63,782	26,013	8,272	15,145	14,013	20,099	7,158
2005	95,655	66,992	25,658	9,595	17,867	13,551	28,663	14,424

[a]The peak number of the total is 100,323 (2003). [b]Typical seven causes of pollutions are air, water, soil, noise, vibration, land subsidence, and smell, among which soil and land subsidence are trivial. The last two totals of percentage distribution are from 0.4 to 0.6, which are omitted from the table
Sources: Environmental Dispute Coordination Committee (1999), Tables 1-4-2 and 1-4-3; (2007), Tables 2-4-2, and 2-4-3

6.3.2 Symbolic Examples

During the rapid economic growth period, there were four examples of the effects of pollution (historical descriptions of the first three are quoted from Tsuru 1993, p. 133). First was the "Kumamoto Minamata disease" case of mercury poisoning. The convulsive deaths of cats and crows in the Minamata area were reported in 1953. The Chisso Company made the first filing of a report to the local health office on "the incident of unexplainable disease" among some residents of Minamata in 1956. Their central nerves were massively damaged. Then, the residents suffered from quadriplegia (the four-limb paralysis) and from optical, hearing, and language disorders. Babies were also included as victims of congenital Minamata disease.[2]

Second was the "itai-itai disease" case of cadmium poisoning in the Toyama prefecture, which was reported in 1955 at the 17th Conference of Surgical Specialists on the existence of a peculiar disease in a certain region along the Jintsu River. The poisoned people suffered tremendous pain such that this disease is called the itaiitai disease (itai means pain in Japanese). Symptoms of cadmium poisoning included kidney trouble and bones that were so fragile that they broke even on moving in bed.

Third was the "Yokkaichi pollution" case of respiratory ailments (breathing illness). Complaints reached the municipal office of Yokkaichi (one of the earliest petrochemical complexes in Japan) in 1959. Fourth was the "second Minamata disease" case of mercury poisoning along the Agano River in the Niigata Prefecture. During the period from August 1964 to July 1965, many patients showed extreme cases of mercury poisoning. There was no decisive cure for these cases of mercury

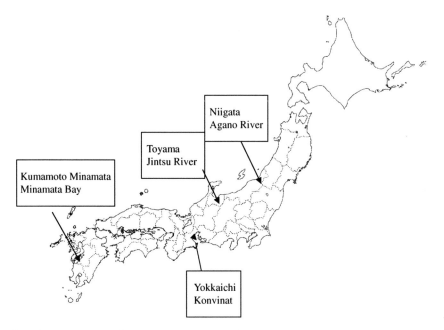

Fig. 6.3 Japanese map of the symbolic examples of the effects of pollution

and cadmium poisoning, so people died. Figure 6.3 shows a Japanese map of the symbolic examples of the effects of pollution.

6.3.3 Countermeasures Taken by the Government

The Japanese government finally took these complaints seriously, and began various countermeasures. It established the Environment Agency belatedly. But it took almost 10–15 years for the official report or the complaints to reach the local government. During these years, the number of victims greatly increased.

The government took the following two important countermeasures: First was an enactment of the Basic Law for Environmental Pollution Control (July 1967). In addition, the United Nations General Assembly called an international conference on the environment (December 1968). In answer to this call, an international symposium of social scientists was held in Tokyo in 1970. As a result, the Tokyo Resolution was introduced that recognized nature's endowment as a part of human rights, which "served as a springboard for a basic reorientation in the matters concerning environmental rights of citizens" (Tsuru 1993, p. 134). Then the Japanese law was revised, to erase the *harmony clause* that meant that harmony with sound economic development should be considered. This revision of the law was very important.

Second was the establishment of the Environment Agency (July 1971, later raised in status to the Ministry of the Environment). The agency was charged with the task of formulating and promoting basic principles about the conservation of the environment, and of coordinating the activities of the administrative agencies.

6.3.4 Antipollution Litigations, Standards, and Investment

Between June 1971 and March 1973, four major pollution (Kogai) trial cases all ended in victory for the plaintiffs. The Stockholm Conference on the Human Environment (held in June 1972) provided a renewed stimulus for antipollution policies and movements in Japan. Antipollution litigations were taken and stricter standards were set. Table 6.2 shows their strictness. Antipollution investment in total expenditure on plant and equipment by private enterprises in percentage greatly increased from 3.0 (1965) to 5.0 (1969), 8.6 (1972), then 18.6 (1975) (Tsuru 1993, p. 137; Environment Agency 1976, Fig. 8).

Table 6.2 Standards for air quality and automobile exhaust—International comparison

	Air quality objectives, 1975[a]				Automobile exhaust standards		
	SO_2 (ppm)	Particulates (mg/m^3)	NO_2 (ppm)	Year applicable	CO (g/km)	HC (g/km)	NO_x (g/km)
Japan	0.04	0.10	0.02	1976	2.10	0.25	0.60
Japan				1978	2.10	0.25	0.25
USA	0.14	0.26	0.13	1975[b]	9.30	0.93	1.93
Canada[c]	0.06	0.12	0.10	Future	2.13	0.25	1.94
France	0.38	0.35	n.a.		n.a.	n.a.	n.a.
Sweden	0.25	n.a.	n.a.	1975	24.2	2.10	1.90
Italy	0.15	0.30	n.a.		n.a.	n.a.	n.a.

[a]All figures are average daily values or their equivalents; [b]Federal government standards; [c]For Ontario
Source: Quoted from Tsuru (1993), Table 5.4, p. 136

As a result of these government countermeasures, major claims to pollution have greatly decreased since the past peak in 1972. Figure 6.4 shows exponential growth of major claims to pollution. In Fig. 6.4, 7-total means the number of claims to seven typical pollutions: that is, air, water, soil, noise, vibration, land subsidence, and smell. The 7-total decreased until 1995, and then again increased up until 2003. A recent increasing trend of claims was caused by the steep increase in air pollution. Another outstanding point is a large increase in the "Others" category (excluding 7-total) where majority claims are waste products. The number of claims to waste products was not so large in the past peak of 1972.

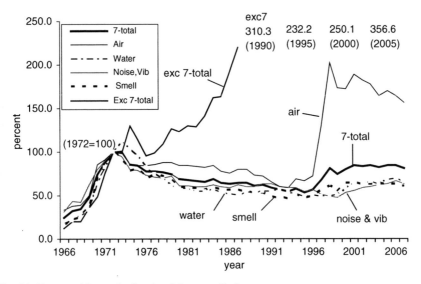

Fig. 6.4 Exponential growth of major claims to pollution.
Sources: The data source of Table 6.1 by the author. Extended by Environmental Dispute Coordination Committee (2009), Tables 2-4-1, 2-4-2 and 2-4-3

6.4   Inflation and People Left Behind by the Advancing Times

6.4.1   Inflation

Japan suffered from a high rate of inflation during the period 1960 to the early 1980s. (see Chapter 2, Fig. 2.2.) Two spikes of inflation were caused by the respective oil shocks of 1973 and 1979. We consider that inflation was more or less a cost of high economic growth that was undesirable because of its adverse effects on income distribution. Inflation is generally advantageous for physical asset holders, for they have capital gains through their asset price increases. Borrowers also gain, for their repayment burden becomes lighter in the process of inflation. However, creditors (lenders) are losers under the high rate of inflation. In particular, bank deposits and savings' real value are weakened under the high rate of inflation, because their interest rate is often lower than the inflation rate. Japanese households' portfolio of financial assets heavily depend on the deposits and savings, with minor portions being invested in equity.

Table 11.2 in Chapter 11 includes the Japanese households' portfolio of financial assets. We observe that the Japanese generally have a strong preference for safety over returns. They held a majority of financial assets as bank deposits (59.3 percent), insurance, and so on (27.5 percent), and securities (13.1 percent) in 2005. These percentage distributions have fluctuated according to the business environment. However, the fundamental property has not largely changed. This means that Japanese households are weak to hedge inflation in particularly high inflationary conditions. (Compared with other countries such as the US and the UK Japanese security holdings are small, varying from 10 to 20 percent reflecting the economic situation.)

Under the high inflation period and despite the high economic growth, non-contributing groups (families) remained in the society: these included the aged, nonworking head of household, and single-mother and children families. These were major recipients of government assistance (by livelihood protection). People on fixed incomes suffered. Pensioners were not receiving the real value of their pension unless it was indexed to the cost of living.[3]

Inflation is generally a serious problem, but since the early 1980s, it has become a less important economic matter in Japan. After the bubble economy collapsed, the deflationary spiral was a more serious matter until recently in 2007.

6.4.2 People Left Behind by the Advancing Times

During the rapid growth period, we observed greater increases of per capita *GDP* and real wages both at annual rate of 7.3 percent (see Table 5.1). However, there were groups of people who did not benefit or poorly benefited from the high economic growth. They were nonworking households (due to the aged, sickness, or injury) and households of the self-employed without an employee(s) and workers working for a small company. (See Planning Bureau of EPA 1975, II, Chapter 2, Section 2, for examples.)

People assisted by livelihood protection (per 1000 population) greatly decreased from 24.4 (1950) to 12.4 (1973) (Japan Statistical Association 2006, Vol. 5, 23–37). The same was true of assisted households (per 1000 households) that decreased from 39.6 (1953) to 21.6 (1973) (NI of PSSR 2009). In this connection, we raise three issues. First, earlier on when the livelihood protection was introduced, the ratio of assisted working households to the total assisted households was high at 58.4 (1958), although it decreased to 26.4 (1973) during the rapid economic growth period (NI of PSSR 2009). We believe that this reflected the existence of low paid workers who were working by the day, doing piecework at home, and working for a small company.

Second, the ratio of assisted people to the total population showed relatively large differences among the prefectures. Figure 6.5 shows assisted ratios (per 1000 population), and *CVs* (coefficient of variance[4]) of per capita income by prefecture and of assisted ratios by prefecture. There are some interesting facts in the figure. During the observation period of rapid economic growth, an equality of income distribution advanced not only on a national economy level (see Fig. 2.4) but also on a prefecture level (Fig. 6.5). Assisted ratios also decreased, but, the *CV* of assisted ratios by prefecture[5] steeply increased until the mid 1960s. This meant that the dispersion of the assisted ratios by prefecture increased. This might partly represent the existence of people who did not benefit or poorly benefited from the rapid economic growth.

Table 6.3 is an enlarged reproduction of Fig. 6.5. Since the end of the rapid economic growth period, assisted ratios declined until 1995 (bottom), and then

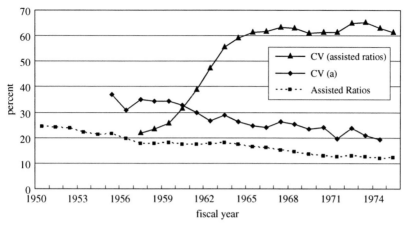

Fig. 6.5 Assisted ratios and coefficient of variance (*CV*(a) and *CV* (assisted ratios)).
Sources: *CV* (assisted ratios) is calculated by ACB on SSS of MCA (1959–76), Table: Assisted households, Persons, Ratios, and Total Population; *CV*(a) is calculated by DNA of ESRI, CAO (b), Data for 1955–1974 downloaded from (www.esri.cao.go.jp/jp/sna/kenmin/68sna_s30/main.html); For assisted ratios, Japan Statistical Association, 2006, Vol. 5, 23–37
Notes: 1. Assisted ratios = assisted persons (per 1000 population) ratio by livelihood protection; 2. *CV* (a) = *CV* of per capita prefectural income

Table 6.3 Assisted ratios and *CVs* (Coefficient of variance)

Year	1950	1955	1960	1965	1970	(1973)	1975	1980	1985	1990	1995	2000	2005
Assisted ratios	24.4	21.6	17.4	16.3	13.0	12.4	12.1	12.2	11.8	8.2	7.0	8.5	11.6
CV (a), (b), (c)	–	36.9	32.7	24.6	24.1	20.9	13.9	14.2	15.2	17.3	13.9	14.0	16.4
CV (assisted ratios)	–	–	21.8 ('57)	61.2	61.3	65.2	55.3	56.3	68.1	61.4	59.0	55.8	55.2

Notes and sources: See Fig. 5.3 for *CV (a)*, *CV (b)* and *CV(c)*; Fig. 6.5 for assisted ratios and *CV* (assisted ratios); *CV* (assisted ratios) for 1980–2005 is obtained from SB of MCA (f) (–2001) and SB of MIAC (g) (–2007)

increased until 2008 (12.5). The difference of local income increased during the bubble economy period (*CV (b)*) and then increased from 2003 (*CV(c)*). The difference of assisted ratios by prefecture has maintained a high percentage even after the end of rapid growth.

Third, an assessment of individual income is difficult (except for employees of corporations), because people more or less want to understate their incomes to the tax office, particularly the self-employed. For employees that work for corporations in Japan, taxes are collected through withholding at their workplace, so that their incomes are almost completely captured by the tax office. By referring to some literature and a government report, Takayama (1980, pp. 97–99) estimated that the number of assisted people's ratio to eligible income group of government aid would be about 10 percent. He explained the reason for the low rate of claims for the government assistance. (1) The system of livelihood protection gave people an image of being a failure in life. (2) Application was very restrictive such that the office and district welfare officers processed various assessments, particularly in the earlier years of the introduction of the system. (3) Publicity of the system by the government was lacking. Tachibanaki and Urakawa (2006, pp. 124–127) also raised similar reasons and their recent estimates of assisted households' ratio to the eligible income households of the government aid were 19.7 (1995), 16.3 (1998), and 16.3 (2001) in percentages.

We observed the negative effects or distortions of the rapid economic growth. As Galbraith mentions, there is an inherent tendency, that causes social imbalance between the supply of privately produced goods and services and those of the state. The negative results mentioned above were more or less caused by social imbalance.

First, overcrowding in metropolitan areas caused social maladies, pollution, congestion, and the high cost of living on the one hand. On the other hand, depopulated areas faced a rapidly aging society and devastated farm lands. To cope with the problem of depopulated areas, the government initiated the Act on Special Measures for Depopulated Areas and spent a great amount of money in the 1970s and again the 1980s. But the problem continued.

Second, the most serious negative effect was environmental disruption, which exploded during the period of rapid economic growth. To cope with the problem, the government belatedly took various countermeasures, such as the enactment of the Basic Law for Environment Pollution Control and the establishment of the Environment Agency. The government then put the regulation into practise and fostered antipollution investment.

Third, Japan suffered from high inflation, which was more or less a cost of the rapid economic growth and distorted income distribution. Japanese household portfolios in general were too weak to hedge inflation, because their financial assets portfolio too heavily depended on bank deposits and savings.

Finally, we raised the question of the people left behind by the advancing times: Those low-income groups whose income are estimated at less than the government aid level. We showed a rapidly increased *CV* of assisted ratios, meaning that differentials of assisted ratios among prefectures greatly increased.

Notes

1. Galbraith raised the following reasons for this: (1) Consumer's desires are produced by producer's clever marketing technique and consumer's vanity, working to the advantage of private production. (2) Public services are based on taxes, but people do not like to accept higher taxes. (3) Continuous inflation deteriorates both the budget of local authorities and the living of the public service employees, causing labor mobility from the public to the private production.

2. A brief history of Kumamoto Minamata disease shows how many years had passed until the disease was confirmed by the Chisso Company and recognized by the government, respectively.
   1932.5 production process starts (factory).
   1956.5 confirmed Minamata disease by the Chisso Company.
   1968.5 stops production process.
   1968.9 The government recognizes Minamata disease as disease caused by pollution.
   1973.7 The suit ends in the victory of plaintiffs.
   1997.7 safety declaration.
   2006.5 The 50-year memorial: designated victims accounted for 2200 people, among which 1500
   died; still under application 3,700 designated victims.
   Source: Nihon Keizai Shinbun (Japanese Economic Newspaper) dated of May 1 2006.
3. Old age pensions were indexed in 1973.
4. See Chapter 5, footnote 3 for the meaning of the coefficient of variance. (The larger the variance, the greater the spread of the series around its mean.)
5. The worst (highest) assisted ratios were four prefectures in Kyushu district and one in the Kochi prefecture in Shikoku district during the observation period 1957–1975. Some of those prefectures in Kyushu district were seriously affected by coal mining closures, which reflected the energy change from coal to oil, particularly the Fukuoka prefecture from around 1960 onward, and then the Nagasaki prefecture, followed by the Kumamoto prefecture.

Chapter 7
Bubble Economy and Its Generation

The Japanese economy survived two oil crises and experienced moderate growth. Inflation settled down and Japan's trade surplus largely widened in the early 1980s. Everything seemed to be going well. The bubble economy evolved and then burst, which brought prolonged stagnation of some 10 years. As a result, the economy had to pay huge penalties. We deal with these matters in this and the next chapter. This chapter deals with the bubble economy and its causes. First, we explain the properties of the bubble. Second, we discuss accumulated causes leading up to the start of the bubble economy, and the triggering role of monetary and fiscal policies.

7.1 Speculative Bubbles

Stock prices began to increase in 1983 and escalated in the following years. Reflecting the increase of office and land demands, real estate prices rose rapidly in Tokyo in 1986. The phenomenon spread over the country from Tokyo to Osaka, then to the Nagoya metropolitan areas, and further to local areas.

Corporations and individuals bought real estate or housing and company stock shares, and these prices escalated. It became almost like a game to obtain capital gains. Participants were involved in a buy-and-sell game, believing that prices would go ever higher. This situation was unsustainable. Transaction prices were too high to be explained by economic rationality. Suddenly, real estate and stock prices rapidly declined (not always concurrently), and then spread rapidly. People were faced with heavy capital losses. This phenomenon is called the bubble economy collapse.

7.1.1 Land and Stock Prices

What is the bubble? Speculative trading and rising prices in shares and real estate swelling much faster than real economic growth characterize the bubble. Figure 7.1 shows how these prices rapidly rose and finally declined. Average share prices rose 4.9 fold (to the peak in 1989) from the year-end price of 1982. During the period from 1983 to 1991, nominal *GDP* grew by a factor of 1.7. During the same period,

M. Iyoda, *Postwar Japanese Economy*, DOI 10.1007/978-1-4419-6332-1_7,
© Springer Science+Business Media, LLC 2010

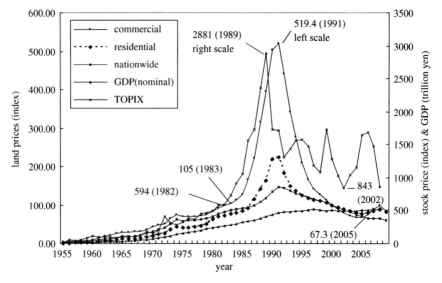

Fig. 7.1 Land and stock prices (Index) and *GDP*.
Sources: Japan Statistical Association (2006), Vol. 3, 15–18 for 1955–2004; Japan Real Estate Institute (2009), Index of Urban Land Price; CAO of GoJ (2008, Japanese ed.), Long Run Economic Statistics for *GDP* and Topix (home page:www5.cao.gov.jp/j-j/wp/wp-je08/08.html)
Notes: 1. Commercial and residential show the land price of commercial and residential use in six major cities, respectively: nationwide shows the all-urban land price average.; 2. Six major city areas: Metropolitan Tokyo (23 wards), Yokohama, Nagoya, Kyoto, Osaka, and Kobe; 3. Land price is the value each year at the end of March (at March-end price 2000 = 100); 4. Topix (Tokyo Stock Price Index at the period-end value) = 100 at the price of January 4, 1968; 5. *GDP* in trillion yen

average land prices of commercial and residential use in six major cities rose 5.0 and 2.9 times, respectively. After the peak, average share prices declined to 45 percent from their peak in 1992. On the other hand, the land prices for commercial and residential use in six major cities continued to decline until 2005, which became 13 and 34 percent (1975 and 1983 levels), respectively, against the peak. Both the nationwide (all urban) and the all urban, except for six major cities, land prices similarly moved, rising 1.7 fold (from 1983 to 1991) and decreasing to 44 and 43 percent (around the 1978 level), respectively, from their peak in 2008.

By observation, we find some properties of the bubble process and the consequence. First, speculative trading and rising stock prices started earlier than real estate, peaking out earlier as well in 1989. Second, land prices for commercial use increased faster and greater than the residential use; accordingly, the decrease of the former prices was also larger than the latter. Third, the nationwide (all urban) land price grew by a factor of 1.7 from 1983 to 1991, equivalent to that of *GDP* (nominal) growth. As far as observing the index, local land prices were not greatly affected in the bubble years. Fourth, after the bubble burst, land prices greatly declined and returned to the mid-1970s levels (an exception was the 1983 level for residential use in six major cities). Table 7.1 articulates some of these outstanding indexes.

Table 7.1 Land and stock prices (index)

Item	Start	Peak	Trough	Peak/start ratio
Stock (Topix)	593.7 (1982)	2881.4 (1989)	843.3 (2002)	4.9
Land (6 major city areas)				
Commercial use	104.6 (1983)	519.4 (1991)	67.3 (2005)	5.0
Residential use	78.8 (1984)	223.4 (1991)	77.6 (2005)	2.8 (2.9)[c]
Land (nationwide)				
All urban	94.1 (1986)	147.8 (1991)	63.9 (2008)	1.6 (1.7)[c]
Other urban[a]	95.0 (1986)	144.9 (1991)	63.4 (2008)	1.5 (1.7)[c]
Reference (GDP nominal)[b]	280.8 (1983)	464.9 (1991)		1.7

[a]Excluding six major city areas. [b]In trillion yen. *GDP* is a reference value that has no relation to "start" and "peak." [c]The ratio of peak to 1983 value is in parentheses. See Fig. 7.1
Sources: See Fig. 7.1

7.1.2 Capital Gains and Losses

Figure 7.2 shows capital gains and losses of land and corporate shares. From 1985 onward, capital gains of corporate shares greatly increased and the cumulative amount since 1985 peaked at 601 trillion yen in 1989. However, it rapidly decreased in 1990 and 1992 due to huge capital losses of 307 and 178 trillion yen, respectively, and almost disappeared until 1998. The same was true of land also. Capital gains

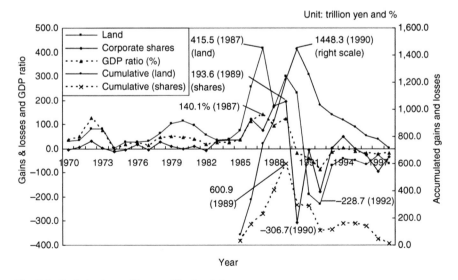

Fig. 7.2 Capital gains and losses of land and shares.
Source: EPA of GoJ (a) (2000), Part 2, I, 3 (Reconciliation Account)
Notes: GDP ratio = Capital gains and losses of land and shares total/*GDP* at current prices. Cumulative gains and losses are from 1985 on

of land greatly increased from 1985, the cumulative amount peaked at 1,448 trillion yen in 1990, and then continuously decreased. The amount was 714 trillion yen (about a half of its peak) in 1998 and was possibly nil in the early 2000s. Table 7.2 articulates some of these outstanding values.

Table 7.2 Capital gains and losses since 1985

	(unit: trillion yen)			
	Annual peak		Cumulative amounts since 1985	
	Gain	Losses	Peak	nil
Shares	193.6 (1989)	−306.7 (1990)	601 (1989)	(1998)
Land	415.5 (1987)	−228.7 (1992)	1,448 (1990)	(early 2000s)

Note and source: See Fig. 7.2

What were the results of the bubble? As far as the capital gains and losses were concerned, as a whole society, it seemed to be a zero sum game for 15–20 years.[1] A huge number of participants (individuals and corporations) had huge gains during the bubble years and lost these gains after the collapse of the bubble, bringing a great number to bankruptcy. Considering the long-term dragged effect, it turned out to be the worst game (in a figurative expression) as members in the society became losers as a whole.

7.2 Backgrounds

7.2.1 Trade Imbalance

Japan's trade surplus[2] expanded enormously from 1981, but the yen–dollar exchange rate showed a decrease (devaluation) until the summer of 1985, though the rate oscillated considerably. The following factors may explain this phenomenon: (1) The Japanese trade surplus was increasing year by year (see Fig. 2.7 in Chapter 2). Japanese exports greatly increased until 1985, but imports stagnated during the period. (2) Under the Reagan administration (1981–1989), the twin deficits (the trade and the finance deficits) continued (see Fig. 7.3). The high US interest rates caused by the financial deficit brought an excess demand for dollars. The interest rate on Treasury bonds exceeded 10 percent for the period 1979–1982, and the US prime rate was far greater than this rate. (see The Council of Economic Advisers 2007, Table B-73.)

High US interest rates were attractive to other currencies. The Japanese yen was converted to US dollars, which contributed to keeping the dollar's high exchange rate and yen's relatively weak exchange rate. Germany also had a huge trade surplus and German marks were also converted to US dollars. However, German marks greatly appreciated during the first half 1980s (Nakamura 1995, p. 252).

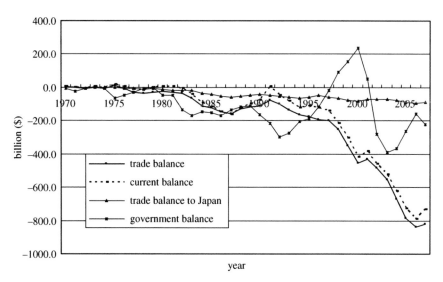

Fig. 7.3 US International trade and government balance.
Sources: Council of Economic Advisers (2009), Appendix B Statistical Tables Relating to Income, Employment, and Production (various editions for the trade balance to Japan)

As mentioned above, the United States had huge deficits in both the government budget and the trade balance of payments in the early 1980s. These situations were not adequate for the balanced development of the world economy. The world's leading financial ministers of the *G5* held a conference called the Plaza Accord[3] and agreed to further the dollar decline to solve the US trade imbalance. As a result, the yen greatly appreciated to 159 yen from 237 yen to the dollar in terms of a monthly closing average during the 10-month period from September to July 1986, which caused a serious blow to Japanese export industries and generated depression. (see RSD of BoJ (a) 1985, p. 263; 1986, p. 263.) Industries hardest hit were the export-oriented electronics, steel, and automobile. A steep appreciation of the yen continued up to 1988, with the annual average yen–dollar rate at 128.2 in 1988.

From the early 1980s, the US trade deficit escalated, while the Japanese trade surplus greatly increased even after the Plaza Accord (see Fig. 2.7 in Chapter 2). Nakamura (1995, p. 255) explains this as follows: (1) The yen had almost doubled in value, but the rise in export prices for the period 1985–1991 was held down to less than 20 percent. (2) The labor productivity index showed massive improvements, helped considerably by the fall in the yen-based prices of imported raw materials, by the overseas production of parts, and by the other strenuous efforts of industries to rationalization. (3) Since the yen was continuously appreciating, new J-curve effects[4] were being generated all the time.

The US trade deficit was largely a result of US trade with Japan (see Fig. 7.3). The Japan–US Structural Impediments Initiative Talks (*SII*, 1989–1990) were held to remove Japanese barriers to free trade in order to improve US access to the Japanese market and to reduce the trade imbalance between the two countries. Japan and the

United States had an agreement and made a report in 1990. Japan agreed to make an effort to adjust the economic structure for international harmony and the United States agreed to clear up its fiscal deficit and to encourage savings and investment.

To cope with the high-yen recession caused by the depressed state of export industries, the Japanese government initiated monetary and fiscal policies aimed at expanding domestic demand.

7.3 The Triggering Role of Monetary, Fiscal, and Other Policies

Table 7.3 shows monetary and fiscal policies and major events from 1983 to 1990. The Bank of Japan gradually reduced the bank rate from 5 percent to 3 percent in November 1986, and then to the historical low rate of 2.5 percent in February 1987. This level continued until the hike to 3.25 percent in May 1989. The general price level remained stable in the late 1980s as import prices of energy and other materials were rather depressed due to the appreciation of the yen and the balance between demand and supply in the world market. The Bank of Japan continued to provide money, which allowed banks and other financial institutions to expand loans for speculative trading in shares and real estate. The money supply increased and grew

Table 7.3 Monetary and financial policies, and major events (1983–1990)

Year	Official interest rate (%) (monetary policy)	Financial policy (unit: trillion yen)	Major events (* denotes a new cabinet)
1983	(10) 5.0		1982(11) Nakasone cabinet*
1985			(9) Plaza Accord
1986	(1) 4.5		(4) Maekawa Report
	(3) 4.0		
	(4) 3.5		
	(11) 3.0		
1987	(2) 2.5 (historical low rate until this time)	(5) 6 Emergency fiscal package	(10) Black Monday
			(11) Takeshita cabinet*
1988			(4) Tax Reform (the non- tax plan for small savings—abolished)
1989	(5) 3.25		(4) Tax reform (consumption tax, etc.)
	(10) 3.75		(6) Uno cabinet*
	(12) 4.25		(8) Kaifu cabinet*
			(11) The Berlin Wall (removed)
			(12) 38,915 yen—Nikkei Stock Average (historical record high)
1990	(3) 5.25		
	(8) 6.0		

Note: Month is in parentheses
Source: IB of EPA (a) (2000), Chronology of main economic events

to double-digit annual rates from 1987 to 1990.[5] As a result, stock prices (the Topix) rose sharply from early 1986 to December 1989, peaking at 2,884 on December 18, 1989; the Nikkei Stock Average peaked at 38,915 yen on December 29.[6]

At the same time, the government implemented a large emergency fiscal package amounting to 6 trillion yen aimed mostly at public investment (May 1987). Local governments were also advised to expand regional development projects. Corporate profits for the non-export-oriented industries rose even during the high-yen recession period (1986), and those for export-oriented industries actually rose in 1987 (Fig. 7.4). Corporate investment greatly increased from 1987 to 1988—a long awaited boom since the first oil crisis. To cope with the shortage of labor, companies installed automated office equipment and industrial robots. (see EPA of GoJ (b) 1989, Chapter 1, Section 3; Nakamura 1995, Chapter 7, Section 6.)

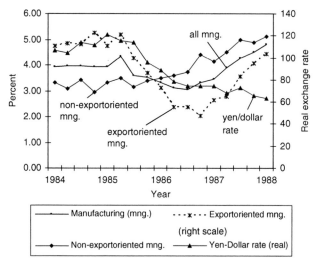

Fig. 7.4 Change in current profit-sales ratio (manufacturing) and real exchange rate, 1984–1988. *Source*: Extracted from EPA of GoJ (b) (1989), Charts 1-3-5 and 2-1-6. Data obtained from *Economic White Paper, 1988 Ed.* (in Japanese)
Note: Index based on June 1973 = 100. GNP deflator deflates real exchange rate.

Consumer demand was also strong and was directed at luxury commodities, such as sophisticated residential units, large passenger cars, jewelry, and upscale branded goods. See EPA of GoJ (b) (1989, pp. 13–16; 1990, pp. 48–53) for a look at the steady household consumption and its diversification and sophistication. This strong growth in consumer demand is known as the wealth effect[7]. People and business firms become more wealthy as a result of capital gains from real estate and stock market investments and land.

For the land bubble, Yoshikawa (2002, p. 69) explains that the land demand was primarily for "office construction in major cities," and for "the development of resorts in the countryside, more luxurious than those that were already in place." The sudden appreciation of these land prices was caused by "higher expected returns, and was not the result of lower interest" (p. 69). Government policies and plans contributed to the formation of these inflated expectations, "which fostered false expectations, and ultimately resulted in massive bad debts" (p. 70). Yoshikawa discusses some examples. The Fourth Comprehensive National Development Plan (1987) positioned Tokyo as an international city, and advocated the development of an exchange network concept with Tokyo at the core. In June 1987, the Resort Law was enacted with the understanding that demand for leisure facilities was increasing.

Providing the impetus was the huge trade surplus, the strong yen rate to the US dollar, and the low interest rates after the Plaza Accord, which caused large money supplies. Reflecting deregulation for financial institutions and capital transactions in the 1980s,[8] firms also had other means of procuring funds from domestic and overseas markets including the Euro market at lower interest rates. Big listed firms (Tokyo Stock Exchange) used direct financing to obtain monetary funds in both domestic and overseas capital markets by issuing new shares, *CB* (convertible bonds), *WB*(warrant bonds) and *SB*(straight bonds) with less expensive costs (Itoh 2000, p. 84). As a result, a large volume fund was invested in stocks, other financial assets, and real estate on the one hand. On the other, it was directed at foreign investment in particular from 1986 onward.

Under these circumstances, large corporations became less dependent on banks. Financial institutions were more conscious of the cost of fund raising than ever before. But on the other hand, the risk management at these financial institutions became weaker, resulting in easy lending for these transactions, particularly for real estate. As a result, domestic borrowers at Japanese banks shifted from being large businesses to "medium and small businesses, especially real estate agencies, construction companies, specialized housing finance companies (nonbanks that did not receive deposits) and individual persons" (Itoh 2000, p. 86). (see also EPA of GoJ (b) 1994, pp. 107–8.)

Market discipline weakened among the market participants. As the EPA of GoJ (b) (1994, p. 148) explains, investors were not aware of the investment risks involved. Security companies and financial institutions failed to provide adequate information about their products in terms of the risks involved, and sold financial products by their own company's policies. Corporations buying these investments were too naive to understand the potential risks.

7.4 A Critical Factor

In an attempt to explain the swelling of the bubble economy, we showed "backgrounds (huge trade surplus and deregulation of financial institutions and capital transactions)," "monetary policy with the low interest rate," "financial policy with a large fiscal package," and "other government policy and plan." All of these factors contributed to the swelling of the Japanese bubble economy.

What critical factor generated the bubble economy? The following is a brief summary of an argument by Ichinose (2005, introductory chapter). He notes three facts that explain the expanding of the Japanese bubble economy. First, Japan's money supply during the bubble period was not particularly high compared with other advanced countries in Europe and North America. Second, the Japanese current balance of payment was a huge surplus, which seemed to be offset by capital exports. Nonetheless, abnormally high yen appreciation continued for 3 years after the Plaza Accord. Third, despite the large scale of capital exports, the bubble economy was generated domestically.

Ichinose questions the major explanations in literature regarding the swelling of the bubble economy from the viewpoint of whether or not they answer the above three questions. He presents the theory of a large influx of short-term capital, particularly "impact loans" as the key to the questions. Impact loans are loans in a foreign currency, mostly in US dollars by foreign exchange banks with no restrictions on the use of the funds.[9] At first, only large corporations and trading corporations used the loans, then construction, real estate, (nonbank) money lending industries, and individuals gradually began to use them. They invested those loans in the asset market, particularly the stock market through specified money trusts and fund trusts managed by trust banks. The borrowing banks included city banks, local banks, mutual loan and savings banks, and credit cooperatives.

Japan introduced short-term funds, not for financing a deficit of overall balance of payments but for domestic and overseas investments. The capital account in the long term was huge deficits but was a surplus in the short term, and the bank's short-term financial account was a large surplus, resulting in increases of foreign exchange reserves for the years 1986–1988. (see Table 7.4). As a result, impact loans also contributed to the continuous appreciation during this period. Impact loans were a major part of short-term loans for domestic management.

Table 7.4 Balance of payments (rearranged table by Ichinose) Unit=100 million US dollars

Year	Current balance	Long–term capital	Short-term capital	Balance of monetary movements (Others)	Errors and omissions	Total= Changes in foreign exchange reserves
1984	350	−497	−43	170	37	18
1985	492	−645	−9	125	40	2
1986	868	−1,315	−16	605	25	157
1987	870	−1,365	239	688	−39	393
1988	796	−1,309	195	452	28	162
1989	572	−892	208	205	−220	−128

Source: Ichinose (2005), Table introductory Chapter 4, rearranged table, p. 19, obtained from RSD of BoJ (a) (1993), 119 Balance of Payments. The author amends this table with minor changes

Short-term impact loans were about 50 billion dollars at the end of 1986, peaking at 226 billion dollars at the end of March 1991. During this period, it increased about 20 trillion yen (170 billion dollars), and the short- and the medium- and long-term Euroyen[10] loans for residents increased by 15 and 8 trillion yen, respectively, the total of which was nearly equivalent to a half of the increase of bank's loan balance related to shares and land (90 trillion yen). The total amount as a result of the impact loans (both short and long term) were 1184.9 (1987), 1722.5 (1988), and 1589.4 (1989) billion dollars.

As Ichinose demonstrated, we recognized that impact loans greatly contributed to the generation of the bubble economy. However, we conclude that the Japanese bubble economy was caused by various factors such as the low interest rate, an inappropriate fiscal package, government policy and plan (contributed to the formation of inflated expectations), and impact loans. All of these factors contributed to the generation and the swelling of the bubble economy. Although the impact loan was a critically important factor, we cannot say that it was the only factor that generated the bubble economy.

7.5 Economic Cost of the Bubble in the Bubble Economy

In this chapter, we defined the bubble economy as the rising prices of shares and real estate beyond which we cannot explain with any economic rationality. We showed the price changes of shares and real estate, and their capital gains and losses. Then we dealt with the background of the bubble and its generating processes. In this section, we discuss the economic cost of the bubble, (see EPA of GoJ (b) 1994, Chapter 2, Section 3.)

First, asset distribution greatly deteriorated (see Fig. 10.1 in Chapter 10). If capital gains are taken into consideration, income distribution also largely deteriorates. Second, housing prices exceeded the purchasing ability of the people who planned to buy houses, causing housing problems (small size, remote area from the workplace, and so on.).

Third, EPA of GoJ (b) (1994, Chapter 2, Section 3) lists five kinds of distortions in the resource allocation that were produced by the bubble. (1) Oversupply of real estate (large-scale land projects such as office building construction and resort development projects). (2) The vigorous activity in asset dealing (*zaitech*)[11] and real estate speculation. (3) Obstruction of investment plans with land acquisitions. (4) Movement in extreme land conservation in major cities (buying the house in remote area, and the attempt to conserve and make skillful use of land). (5) Excess investment and consumption (consumption and investment activity exceeded normal limits).

In the next chapter, we deal with the collapse of the bubble and its consequences (serious economic cost after the bubble burst). We explain the reason for the prolonged stagnation and discuss some lessons learned from the experience of the Japanese bubble economy in Chapter 9.

Notes

1. A zero sum game is a game (in Game Theory) in which one player's gain is equal to others' losses, whatever strategy is taken.
2. Facing the increasing trade imbalances, Prime Minister Nakasone formed a commission headed by the former chairman of the Bank of Japan, Haruo Maekawa. The Maekawa Commission issued a report in April 1986, recommending that Japan should transform its

economic structure from an export-dependent one to one that is domestic-demand oriented. Recommended policies were expansion of domestic demand, tax reform, import promotion of agricultural product, promotion of international policy coordination, and so on (Kanamori et al. (eds.) 2002).

3. The representative of five major industrialized countries (G5) met at New York's Plaza Hotel in September 1985, reaching an agreement called the "Plaza Accord." The G5 was a conference of financial ministers and central bank governors whose member nations were the United States, Germany, France, Japan, and the United Kingdom.

4. The J-curve effect: The immediate potential effect of devaluation of the exchange rate is to raise import prices and to reduce export prices. As a result, the balance of payments could worsen in the short run before the effects of the change induce the longer-term expansion of exports and a cut in imports that would improve the balance of payments. This is because the full adjustment of trade volumes to changing currency devaluation takes time. Letting time be a horizontal axis and the trade surplus a vertical axis, the trade surplus depicts a J-curve for devaluation. For revaluation, the chart shows an inverse-J-curve.

5. Change in average outstanding $M_2 + CD$ from a year ago (RSD of BoJ (a) 1996, Table 3).

6. Topix (the Tokyo Stock Price Index) and the Nikkei Stock Average (the Nikkei Index) are the two major price indexes of the Tokyo Stock Exchange. The Topix, introduced in 1969, is a composite index of all stocks listed on the first section of the Tokyo Stock Exchange. The Nikkei Stock Average was introduced in 1950 by Nihon Keizai Shinbun, Inc. (publisher of Japan's leading business newspaper), and gives 225 stock averages selected from 1727 stocks listed on the first section of the Tokyo Stock Exchange (at the end of 2007). (See Hsu 1999, pp. 426–7; Tokyo Stock Exchange 2008.) These two indexes cover different stocks, but they show similar trends. Note that Fig. 7.1 shows Topix.

7. Wealth effect is the effect on current consumption due to changes in a person's wealth such as owning real estate or investing in the stock market. See the wealth effect on private consumption for EPA of GoJ (b) (1992, Chapter 2; Section 2; and 1993, Chapter 2, Section 4, 2). The effect of financial assets on consumption was significant but not for real estate (owner-occupied houses) because most real estate owned by households in Japan is for dwelling purposes only, and is inherited by the following generation. In this case, capital gains will not be generated.

8. Some examples are as follows: The Foreign Exchange and Foreign Trade Control Law that was revised in 1980 eased foreign exchange controls and made it possible for both residents and nonresidents to invest in domestic and overseas markets (Hsu, 1999, p. 170, 189). The first comprehensive revision of the Banking Act since 1927 was made in 1981, which permitted banks to sell and deal in government bonds. The deregulation particularly in the mid-1980s resulted in the following: the acquisition of commercial papers (CPs) and negotiable certificates of deposit (CDs) issued overseas was permitted for investors; the issuance of the Euroyen CDwas allowed for overseas branches of Japanese banks; foreign currency-denominated convertible bonds were issued by banks in overseas market, and so on. (Hsu 1999, p. 32, 170). Business firms and financial institutions took advantage of these circumstances and made speculative transactions to obtain tremendous financial gains called "Zaitech." Zaitech greatly accelerated the bubble in the prices of shares and land. These businesses and institutions obtained huge gains by trading in domestic and overseas financial assets and real estate investments (Itoh, 2000, p. 82, 84).

9. Impact loan is an English word coined in Japan. At first, impact loans were not allowed to be converted into yen but were deregulated in June 1984, though the regulation on bank's total foreign exchange position remained until 1998. There are short- and long-term loans. The firm who borrowed an impact loan from a bank would immediately sell the borrowed dollar to the bank and used the converted money (yen) for domestic purposes. (see Ichinose 1999, pp. 12–14.)

10. Euroyen is yen circulating outside of Japan (in the Euro-currency market).

11. Zaitech is the active investment of funds in securities, bonds, and so on to increase business profits.

Chapter 8
Bursting the Bubble and Its Consequences

This chapter deals with bursting the bubble and its consequences. First, we follow the "bursting-the-bubble" process. Second, we explain serious consequences brought by the collapse of bubbles; that is (1) the relocation of the factories abroad (industrial hollowing-out), (2) huge nonperforming loans (*NPLs*) in Japanese banks, and (3) financial crisis (outstanding government bonds). Third, we deal with the causes of prolonged stagnation and its results, including "stock adjustments" and "adjustment to worldwide globalization."

8.1 The Process of Bursting the Bubble

8.1.1 Domestic Ground

Despite the increase in stock and land prices, interest rates remained low at 2.50 percent in February 1987. The Bank of Japan raised the rate to 3.25 percent in May 1989, and in stages to 6 percent in August 1990[1] (see Table 7.3). The increase in interest rates affected the stock prices. The average stock price (Topix and the Nikkei average as well) peaked in December 1989 and fell 40 percent in 1990, and the capital loss estimate was about 307 trillion yen; stock prices fell to 45 percent of their peak in 1992 and the capital loss estimate was 178 trillion yen in the year (see Figs. 7.1 and 7.2).

Land prices increased until March 1990, when "the Ministry of Finance introduced 'real estate loans restrictions' that forced financial institutions to submit monthly reports of their real estate loans and to limit the increase in such lending to a level below the rate of increase in their overall lending" (Nakamura 1995, p. 272). Land prices declined and became conspicuous in 1992. Reflecting this decline, the capital loss estimate for land was also enormous, at 189 and 229 trillion yen in 1991 and 1992, respectively. The land price average became 47 percent of its peak in six major cities by 1996 (Figs. 7.1 and 7.2). Latent capital gains (from the shares) and money funds obtained by business firms and financial institutions through equity finance in the course of the bubble gradually melted away.

M. Iyoda, *Postwar Japanese Economy*, DOI 10.1007/978-1-4419-6332-1_8,
© Springer Science+Business Media, LLC 2010

Banks and financial institutions gradually began to see a decline in their own capital ratio to total assets, but in order to continue their international activities, they had to follow the *BIS* Barzel agreement[2] to keep this ratio above 8 percent after April 1993. They restrained loans to clear this ratio, which exacerbated the credit crunch and caused difficulty for many firms particularly medium and small firms.

From spring 1991 onward, the following phenomena appeared: (See Itoh 2000, pp. 90–91; EPA of GoJ (b) 1995, Chapter 1.) (1) Office and real estate demand, purchase of residential units, and the membership of golf clubs began to contract and the prices declined. (2) Consumer demand for goods cooled down. Then the employment condition became severe and growth in real wages stagnated in 1992 and 1993. (3) Overcapacity in the Japanese manufacturing industry was revealed. Japanese firms again intensified attempts to export. As the trade surplus increased, the yen appreciated sharply.

8.1.2 *International Ground*

The appreciation of the yen created serious difficulties for Japanese export industries. The Japanese exchange rate was 145 yen to the dollar in 1990 and appreciated to 102 yen (annual average) in 1994. The dollar was shaken after the monetary and financial crises of the North American Foreign Trade Agreement (*NAFTA*),[3] and yen rate to dollar peaked at 79.75 yen in April 1995 (see Fig. 2.7 in Chapter 2). This caused serious difficulties for Japanese export industries which encouraged the transfer of factories abroad, leading to the industrial hollowing-out of Japan (Itoh 2000, p. 91).

These domestic and international circumstances deepened Japanese depression.

8.2 Consequences of Bursting the Bubble

8.2.1 *Accelerated "Hollowing Out"*

After the bubble collapsed, the yen greatly appreciated, which accelerated the industrial hollowing out of Japan.

The "hollowing out" closely relates to fluctuations in the exchange rate. EPA of GoJ (b) (1995, pp. 256–7) explains three main aspects of the so-called hollowing out phenomenon. The first aspect is the severe competition between domestic products and imports. If domestic manufacturers lose their competitive strength, domestic production would be gradually replaced by imports. The second aspect is that export-oriented domestic production would be replaced by overseas production. As the export process becomes less profitable and local (overseas) production more advantageous, companies will shift their production centers overseas and expand local production activities. The third aspect is that the manufacturing industry would be replaced by the nonmanufacturing industry. As domestic product is replaced by imports and overseas production, the domestic production of the manufacturing industries would shrink, and the shares of less productive nonmanufacturing industry would rise.

Figure 8.1 shows Japanese overseas development. By observation, in the early 1990s, three variables increased side by side: that is, the import penetration ratio (mining and manufacturing), overseas production ratio (manufacturing), and the ratio of investment in overseas facilities. Appreciation of the yen and stagnated domestic condition of the Japanese economy might compel manufacturers to do the hollowing out.[4]

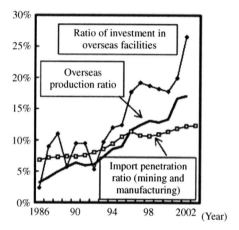

Fig. 8.1 Japanese overseas development.
Sources: Ministry of Finance, *Monthly Financial Review* and *Annual Statistics of Corporations by Industry*; Ministry of Economy, Trade and Industry, *Basic Survey of Overseas Business Activity* and *Aggregate Supply Table*. This figure is copied from CAO of GoJ (2004), Fig. 3-2-1
Notes: 1. Overseas production ratio (for all Japanese companies) = Overseas subsidiaries' (manufacturing) sales amount/Domestic sales amount (manufacturing); 2. Ratio of investment in overseas facilities = Amount invested in facilities of overseas subsidiaries/Amount invested in facilities in Japan; 3. Import penetration ratio (mining and manufacturing) = Import-weight/Aggregate supply-weight

8.2.2 Nonperforming Loans in Japanese Banks

Nonperforming loans (*NPLs*) as defined by the Financial Reconstruction Law (1998) includes "Bankrupt or De Facto Bankrupt," "Doubtful," and "Risk Management" loans that must be exposed. Figure 8.2 shows the Japanese *NPLs*. *NPLs* became widespread in 1993 and increased until fiscal year 2001 (the Japanese fiscal year starts in April and ends in March of the following year), peaking at 52.4 trillion yen at the end of March 2002. Then these amounts decreased and critical period nearly ended in *FY* 2003, at which time cumulative disposal from 1993 exceeded 100 trillion yen.

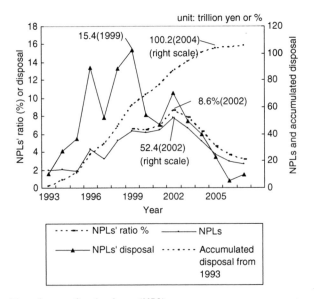

Fig. 8.2 Transition of nonperforming loans (*NPL*).
Sources: FSA, Japanese Government (2008) (Homepage, Table 1); FSA, Japanese Government
(1998)
Notes: 1. All data are at March-end values each year. *NPLs*' disposal figures are preceding years; 2.
NPLs ratio = *NPLs*/Total credit; 3. *NPLs* for 1998 onward based on the Financial Reconstruction
Law and 1993–1997 are based on each financial institution's own estimates, and those for (1993–
1995) include only major banks. There is no continuity in a series of data; 4. *NPLs*' loss disposal
for (1993–1997) is for all banks, and that for 1998 is for all deposit-taking financial institutions. Cumulated disposal for 1993–1998 excludes that of cooperative financial institutions, so
that cumulative disposal for 1999 does not include the losses of those institutions during the period
1993–1998

The Bank of Japan lowered the official interest rate to mitigate the difficulties of
banks and other financial institutions that had bad loans. To maintain the 8 percent
BIS regulation, these institutions had to reduce their loans to preserve their total
assets (see Table 8.1).

The credit crunch affected not only real estate businesses but also the activities of
medium and small firms. The crunch caused a vicious circle between asset deflation
and financial instability, as a result of the *NPLs*. Furthermore, the Asian currency
crisis[5] in 1997 intensified Japanese economic difficulties.

As the economy seemed to recover slowly, the Hashimoto government decided
to reduce the accumulated budget deficits by raising the consumption tax from three
to five percent. Prior to the tax increase in April 1997, people rushed to make purchases such as houses, cars, and other durable consumer goods. As a repercussion,
there was a large decline in domestic demand. With the weak economy and the
growing *NPLs*, the Asian financial crisis erupted in July. The crisis began with
the sudden depreciation of Thai baht, which spread to the Philippines, Malaysia,
Indonesia, and the neighboring countries; the hardest hit was the Korean won whose

Table 8.1 Monetary and Fiscal policies and major events (1991–2008)

Year	Official interest rate (%) (monetary policy)	Fiscal policy (unit: trillion yen)	Major events (* denotes a new cabinet)
1991	(6) Window Operation abolished (7) 5.5 (10) Reserve Requirement Ratio decreased (11) 5.0 (12) 4.5		(1) The Gulf War (11) Miyazawa cabinet*
1992	(4) 3.75 (7) 3.25	(8) 10.7 Comprehensive Fiscal Package	
1993	(2) 2.25 (9) 1.75	(4) 13.2 Comprehensive Fiscal Package (9) 6.15 Emergency Fiscal Package (excl. tax reduction)	(8) Hosokawa cabinet* (4) 8% BIS Regulation
1994		(2) 15.25 Comprehensive Fiscal Package (including 5.47 tax reduction) (10) 630 Public Investment Basic Plan for Fiscal Years 1995–2004	(4) Hata cabinet* (6) Murayama cabinet*
1995	(4) 1.0 (9) 0.5	(9) 14.22 Fiscal Package	(1) WTO launched (4) 79.75 yen-dollar rate (historical record low)
1996		(12) 51.5 Five Year Plan for Public Investment-related	(1) Hashimoto Cabinet* (12) Structural Reform Plan
1997			(4) Consumption Tax Rate (raised to 5%) (12) 2(trillion yen) Special Tax Cut

Table 8.1 (continued)

Year	Official interest rate (%) (monetary policy)	Fiscal policy (unit: trillion yen)	Major events (* denotes a new cabinet)
1998	(6) Monetary System Reform Law; Financial Supervisory Agency launched (10) Financial Reconstruction Law	(4) 16.65 Comprehensive Fiscal Package (11) 17 Emergency Fiscal Package	(7) Obuchi cabinet*
1999	(2) The so-called Zero Interest Rate Policy (the target call rate lowered to 0.15%, subsequently to move as low as possible) (3) 7.4592 trillion yen (injection of capital to 15 major banks)	(11) 18 Economy Renewal Fiscal Package	
2000	(7) Financial Services Agency[a] launched (8) Zero Interest Rate Policy (lifted) (target call rate raised to 0.25)	(10) 11 Fiscal Package	(4) Mori cabinet*
2001	(2) 0.35 (3) 0.25 Zero Interest Rate (reinstated); easy money policy with a quantitative target for the outstanding balance of current accounts at the BoJ (5 trillion yen) (8) 6 trillion yen (the target) (9) 0.1; above 6 allowed; (12) 10–15 (the target range, trillion yen)		(4) Koizumi cabinet* ("no-holds-barred" Structural Reform) (9) 11 September Terrorist Attacks

Table 8.1 (continued)

Year	Official interest rate (%) (monetary policy)	Fiscal policy (unit: trillion yen)	Major events (* denotes a new cabinet)
2002	(2) above 15 allowed (the target range) (9) BoJ purchases shares held by banks (2.18 trillion yen purchased till (9) 2004) (10) 15–20 (the target range)		(10) The Industry Revitalization Corporation (established) (12) 8,300 yen—Nikkei Stock Average (lowest after the bubble burst)
2003	(3) above 20 allowed; (4) 17– 22, 22–27; (5) 27–30; (10) 27–32 (the target range)		(2) Toshihiko Fukui (BoJ Governor)
2004	(1) 30–35 (the target range)		
2005	(5) below 30 allowed (the target range)		
2006	(3) Quantitative Easing ended: 6 trillion yen deposits mandated by the reserve requirement (7) 0.4; Zero Interest Rate Policy ended; the target call rate raised to 0.25%		(9) Abe cabinet*
2007	(2) 0.75; the target call rate, 0.5		(9) Fukuda cabinet*
2008	(10) 0.5; the target call rate, 0.3 (12) 0.3; the target call rate, 0.1	(8) 11.5 Emergency Comprehensive Fiscal Package; (10) 26.9 Fiscal Package (Livelihood Suppport); (12) 37 Emergency Fiscal Package	(9) Aso cabinet*

[a]Financial Supervisory Agency and Financial System Planning Bureau of the Ministry of Finance were integrated

Note: Month is in parentheses

Sources: IB of EPA (a) (2000) and ESRI of CAO (b) (2001–2004), Chronology of main economic events; OECD (–2004), Annex Chronology of main economic events; EPA of GoJ (b) (–2001, English ed.); CAO of GoJ (2002–2007). Fukuda (ed.) (2009)

value fell to less than half of the US dollar in November 1997. As a result, stock prices fell about one-third from June to October 1997. The decline in stock prices sharply increased the bad debt burden of large banks and other financial institutions. Hokkaido Takushoku Bank (the leading bank in the Hokkaido region), Yamaichi Securities (then one of the four biggest securities), Sanyo Securities, and Tokuyo City Bank failed in 1997. (see Fig. 7.1 for the stock price fluctuations after the bubble burst and Fig. 8.2 for the increasing *NPLs*; Koshiro 2000, p. 155–6.)

The government deployed a huge amount of public money in an attempt to rescue banks and other financial institutions, applying the "too big to fail policy." In 1996, 685 billion yen was injected into seven *Jusens*—specialized housing loan companies. The government finally injected public money into banks and other financial institutions in February 1998 in order to recapitalize them and to safeguard the depositors of failed banks;[6] 30 trillion yen was allowed in the beginning, and then raised to 60 trillion yen in the same year (expanded to 70 trillion yen in 2000).

8.2.3 Outstanding Government Bonds (GB)

As a result of the government policies mentioned above, outstanding supply of government bonds greatly increased. Japan fell into fiscal crisis. Figure 8.3 shows outstanding government bonds. The figure shows how much they have increased since the bubble burst in the early 1990s. After the Plaza Accord, the national debt service payments ratio has been about 20 percent. Since the bubble burst, the dependency rate of *GB* issue to general accounts increased and exceeded 40 percent in

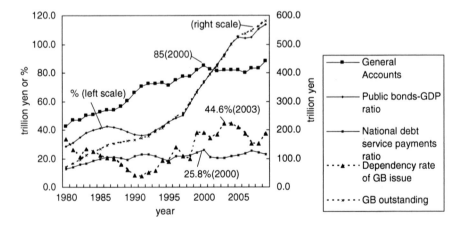

Fig. 8.3 Transition of the general accounts and debts of the government.
Source: Hayashi (ed.) (2007), sources, Table 11). and 13; Extended by Fukuda (ed.) (2009), Figure-Tables I.3.1, I.3.6, II.2.7 and II.2.8
Notes: 1. General Accounts and national debt service payments are based on the initial budget. All data are in terms of fiscal year; 2. National debt service payments ratio = National debt service payments/General accounts; 3. Dependency rate of *GB* issue = *GB* issue/General Accounts; 4. *GB* outstanding (actual budget, but initial for 2008 and 2009); 5. *GDP* is actual results except for outlooks in 2008 and 2009

2003. As a result, *GB* outstanding amounted to 581 trillion yen of public bonds and some 26 trillion yen of the long-term borrowing (March-end 2010, government outlook). Adding the outstanding long-term debt of the local government, the public debt (of central and local governments) totaled 804 trillion yen. Until recently, the rate of increase of both the public bonds-*GDP* ratio and *GB* outstanding was almost the same. Therefore, the *GB* outstanding (581)-tax revenue (46.1) ratio was about 12.6 times. (See Fukuda (ed.) 2009, Figure-Tables I.3.1, I.3.3 and I.3.6.)

The fiscal crisis was caused by government policies. First, public expenditure to cope with the financial crisis did not effectively work. Second, a tremendous amount of public money was injected into banks and other financial institutions as mentioned above. Third, national defense and Official Development Assistance (*ODA*) budgets continued to increase since the 1980s. National defense was nearly 1 percent of *GDP*, and the *ODA* budget in 1995 was 14.5 billion US dollars (almost twice as much as that of the United States and Germany). In 1991–2000 Japan had the largest budget in the world. The US budget surpassed Japan in 2001 and has been the largest since then. In the mid-2000s, Japan was in the second group together with the United Kingdom, France, and Germany. (See Ikeda (ed.) 2008, Figure-Table II.6.3, p. 156.)

Neither the monetary policy of low interest rates nor the fiscal policy of expanding public investment has succeeded in bringing about economic recovery.

Let us observe monetary and fiscal policies as shown in Table 8.1. After the bubble collapsed, in order to mitigate the difficulties of banks and other financial institutions, BoJ gradually lowered the official bank rate from 6 percent in 1991 to 0.5 percent (September 1995). (1) Finally, BoJ introduced the so-called Zero Interest Rate Policy[7] and lowered the target call rate to a low 0.15 percent in February 1999. The Zero Interest Rate Policy was lifted briefly between August 2000 and March 2001, and then reinstated in March 2001, and the official bank rate was reduced to 0.25 percent, then to 0.1 percent (September 2001). (2) BoJ introduced an easy money policy with a quantitative target rate for the outstanding balance of current accounts at the BoJ. The target rate gradually rose in stages from five trillion yen (March 2001), to 30–35 trillion yen (January 2004). The quantitative easing policy finally ended in March 2006. Thereafter, the Zero Interest Policy also ended in July 2006 and the official interest rate rose to 0.4 percent.

In an effort to stimulate the economy, the government introduced nine comprehensive and emergency fiscal packages one after another during the period 1992–2000. The package totals amounted to 122 trillion yen. During this period, economy stagnated and the government mostly financed the budget deficit by issuing bonds.

8.3 Causes of Prolonged Stagnation

After the bubble economy collapsed in 1991, stagnation set in, lasting through 2001. It was only in early 2002 that the Japanese prolonged stagnation period ended. What was the reason for the prolonged stagnation? We examine the several reasons.

First, the bursting of the bubble compelled business corporations, financial corporations, and households to make great "asset adjustments." However, many economists and the policy authorities failed to recognize the seriousness of "stock adjustments." Stock adjustment meant removing excessive debts and writing off nonperforming loans. (Nakatani 2007, Chapter 16). Second, the potential rate of growth was greatly affected by the declining (a) labor force, (b) capital accumulation = savings, and (c) total factor productivity (Supply side economics).[8] (EPA of GoJ (b) 1999, Chapter 2.)

Third, the saturation of demand of individual products and industries caused a long-term deceleration in demand growth (Demand side economics—Keynesians). (Yoshikawa 2002, Chapter 7). Fourth, there was "the lack of profitable investment opportunities due to a high cost structure rather than weak consumption or weak residential construction caused by high real interest rates or a lack of credit." (Sakakibara 2003, p. viii) (Structural reformist advocates).

Fifth, the Japanese economic and social structure could not adjust to "globalization" (Kosai 2007); that is, broad adjustments ranging from production, marketing, and management to systemic adjustments. Finally, the *Economist* (2008) ran a special article entitled "*Japain,* why Japan keeps failing," suggesting that politics and the political leadership of Abe, Fukuda, and Ozawa were the problem. In fact, there were 10 changes in cabinets from Uno in 1989 to Koizumi in 2001. This showed political instability in Japan. We observed during this period that important political and policy decisions were often postponed, exacerbating already serious economic, social, and political problems.

All of these above mentioned explanations may have played a role in prolonging the Japanese stagnation; however, in my opinion, the following two might be the most important causes.

8.3.1 Stock Adjustments

Many economists and the policy authorities failed to recognize the seriousness of "stock adjustments." Many Japanese believed that the real estate prices would always appreciate except perhaps for a short period. Business firms, financial institutions, and households waited for a couple of years, believing that real estate prices would increase and solve the stock problem. However land prices continued to decline. Business firms and financial institutions had maintained huge capital gains (from land and the shares) and money funds obtained through equity financing during the bubble institutions economy, gradually began to melt away. Facing the continuous decline in land prices, these institutions gradually recognized the necessity of stock adjustments.

As a result, the huge cumulative capital gains from stock and land investments during the bubble years became essentially worthless in 1998 for stocks and possibly in the early 2000s for land (see Fig. 7.2). On the other hand, *NPLs* was increasing until the 2001 fiscal year (at the end of March 2002). The *NPLs* ratio registered a peak of 8.6 percent at the end of March 2002 (see Fig. 8.2). Takenaka (2008) raised the obvious striking fact. "It would be impossible for economic revitalization to occur simply by expanding the fiscal deficit as a temporary stop-gap measure, unless the non-performing loans of the banking sector were first resolved" (p. iii). This was also recognition of Mr. Koizumi's administration. (See various fiscal packages in Table 8.1 and debts of the government in Fig. 8.3.)

8.3.2 Adjustment to Worldwide Globalization

The other possible explanation for the prolonged stagnation is Japan's poor adjustment to worldwide globalization. After the first oil crisis, the Japanese economy was so successful in the late 1970s and the 1980s that its system was considered to be exceptional. After the bubble burst, the Japanese economy gradually became rather inward-oriented to cope with the economic difficulties. The Japanese economic and social structures could not effectively adjust to "globalization," particularly during the 1990s. When the Koizumi cabinet was launched in April 2001, Prime Minister Koizumi resolutely proposed "no-holds-barred" reform. Worldwide globalization connected with information technology demanded changes in the Japanese labor–management relationship and in business strategies.

First, the Japanese style of labor management, which consisted of lifetime employment, the seniority wage system, and enterprise unions, caused some difficulties. (See a footnote in Section 3.1 for the Japanese style of labor management.) Under the system, the lay off of regular workers was not easy and labor cost adjustments were not flexible when companies faced changes such as economic slumps. To reduce wages, companies gradually changed from the seniority wage system to a result-oriented pay system. They also tried to employ low-cost nonregular workers (staffs), such as part-timers and others (dispatched workers from temporary labor agencies, contract employees, and others). Figure 8.4 shows that the use of nonregular workers greatly increased from 19.8 (1991) to 34.1 (2008) percent, among which part-timers increased until 2001 and then became steady, and *vice versa* for others. Others were steady until 2001, and then largely increased.[9] When it was possible, companies replaced regular workers with nonregular workers.

Second, Japanese companies particularly the larger ones had multibusiness strategies, under which their affiliated companies ran some businesses. In rapidly growing markets, this strategy would be efficient. However, after the bubble burst and with the domestic market stagnating, lower-priced goods were largely imported from the global market. Japanese companies were now faced with the difficulty of keeping their business structure intact. To overcome this hardship, business restructuring[10] was needed. Companies selected comparatively competitive departments (growing and highly profitable businesses) and invested their capital and human resources into these departments, while, selling, closing, or integrating the less competitive departments.

Thus, in order for Japan to adjust to worldwide globalization and the newly developing information technology age, the Japanese labor management system and business strategies needed to undergo profound changes. These changes had

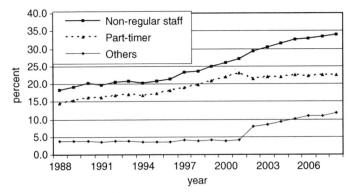

Fig. 8.4 Nonregular staffs (workers).
Sources: (www.stat.go.jp/data/roudou/longtime/03roudou.htm) Historical data 10
Notes: 1. The ratio of nonregular staff, part-timers, and others to employees excluding executives of company or corporation; 2. Part-timer = part-time worker + arbeit (The data have no one accurate classification, depending on the individual company's usage); others = dispatched worker from temporary labor agency + contracted employee or entrusted employee + other; 3. Data for 1988–2001 are as of February each year obtained from *The Special Survey of the Labor Force Survey*; for 2002–2008 annual averages obtained from *The Labor Force Survey (Detailed Tabulation)*

been needed for a long time. In addition, it was fundamentally difficult for the Japanese government to depart from conventional policies to take on socioeconomic reforms. Because, those industries and companies with vested interests developed powerful connections with politicians, and these groups largely supported the government. When the Koizumi cabinet was launched in April 2001, the Prime Minister resolutely proposed a "no-holds-barred" reform.

To reduce the high labor cost, companies shifted their pay system to a result-oriented one called *seikashugi*. Attempts at abolishing, reconsidering, or readjusting the system have been under way since 2000. However the new system has various drawbacks. Target setting for individual personnel assessments was difficult, because employees set easy and short-term performance levels for themselves. Then team cooperation among workers was lost and there was sufficient training on the job for the new employees. By introducing this new system, companies sought to reduce total labor costs but instead it brought discontent among employees. The combined effect of these drawbacks has brought poor business performances in marketing, technology development, and so on.

A survey carried out by the Japan Federation of Economic Organization (*JFEO*) on a management analysis of good companies demonstrated that "longer the average working years of employees, higher the profitability." The study surveyed financial data of listed manufacturing companies during the past 10 years. The above tendency was observed in 7 out of 11 manufacturing industries. The survey also demonstrated that arrangement or integration of affiliated companies contributed to improved profitability, which was observed in 8 out of 11 manufacturing industries. The survey suggested that giving importance to long-term employment, promoting research and development, business concentration to nucleus (company's core) department, and so on were important to improving profitability. (See Nihon Keizai Shinbun [Japanese Economic Newspaper] dated of May 3rd 2004, "Lifetime Employment Contributed to Profitability.")

Notes

1. Nakamura (1995) addresses the *BoJ*'s sluggish attitude: (1) General prices had been affected by lower import prices; (2) BoJ probably wanted to maintain differences between Japanese and US interest rates; (3) The New York stock market crashed in October 1987 ("Black Monday") (p. 272).

2. *BIS's* capital regulations, aimed at the soundness of management and fair competition, are set by Bank for International Settlements (*BIS*) for international banks. That is, international banks must maintain a ratio of at least 8 percent of owned capital against total capital, and domestic banks at least 4 percent.

3. *NAFTA* is an agreement reached by the *United States*, Canada, and Mexico in 1994 to essentially provide an economic bloc to the *EU*.

4. The fluctuation in the exchange rate is the important decision factor of direct foreign investment; however, it is not the only factor. During the latter half of the 1980s, direct overseas investment by the Japanese manufacturing industries were aimed at avoiding trade friction between Japan and North America and taking advantage of the unification of the European market. For North America and the EC, major industries for direct investment were electrical machinery (with equipment and supplies), transport equipment, machinery, and so on. Direct investment in Asia however was aimed at producing goods at low cost and making the supply base for the world market (EPA of GoJ (b) 1995, Chapter 3, Section 1.1).
Based on the survey data, CAO of GoJ (2004, p. 197) notes, "Beginning in the 1990s, growth was evident in investment resulting from greater vertical specialization in the East Asian region, mainly in transport equipment and electrical machinery, as well as investment aimed at market reorganization, primarily in financial institutions."

5. Itoh (2000) explained that Asian monetary crisis was not caused by the deterioration of the current balance of international payment due to poor domestic macroeconomic performance that had occurred in other developing countries such as those of Latin America in the early 1980s. "Most Asian countries that fell [a] prey to this contagious crisis had linked their currencies to the US dollar at fixed rates" (p. 129).

6. The Monetary System Reform was enacted and the Financial Supervisory Agency was launched. The Financial Reconstruction Law was also enacted in 1998 (see Table 8.1).

7. The Zero Interest Rate Policy was meant to make the loan interest rates as low as possible by using the (unconditional) target call rate. When this policy was reinstated in 2001, BoJ also introduced the Lombard-type lending facility, which lent money on security at the official bank rate.

8. *Supply side economics* has the view that economic growth depends on factors affecting supply rather demand, proposing system reforms of tax, restrictive practices, social security, and so on. This is contrasted with the view in *demand side economics* (alternative term of Keynesian economics) that emphasizes the importance of aggregate demand in the economy.

9. Data sources are different between 1988 and 2001 and 2002 and 2008. We should be careful about the time series comparison, but we can see the trend using this figure. An increase of others was caused by the recent revision of the following laws: (1) The Manpower Dispatching Business Law was enacted in 1985, which was at first restrictive. By the 1999 revision, the manpower dispatching became free in principle, and was further relaxed in 2004. (2) The revised Older Persons' Employment Stabilization Law (effective in 2006) stipulated the extension in the retirement age, in stages to 65 (until 2013).

10. Restructuring means changing the business structure by cutting or contracting less profitable business and then promoting growing and highly profitable businesses. This includes arrangement or integration of affiliated companies.

Chapter 9
Toward a Welfare-Oriented Society: Some Lessons from Rapid Economic Growth and the Bubble Economy

This chapter deals with some lessons from rapid economic growth and the bubble economy. After World War II, economic growth was one of Japan's focal points: The country sought to rebuild its ruined national economy, solve its unemployment problems, and boost its growth performance standing between the Western and Eastern Blocks (for developing countries paid attention to the performance between the two economic systems). In this context, countries vied with each other to have superior economic growth, which signified political success. In the early stages, Germany and Italy and then Japan became highly successful economic growth stories and were often called economic miracles.

Japan was the most successful country with respect to growth. As a result, macroeconomic performances were excellent on the one hand, with high income (attained), income equality, low unemployment rate, high spreading rate of durable consumer goods, improvement of social security and infrastructure, and so on. On the other hand, there were negative results such as congestion and depopulated areas, pollution, social imbalance, inflation, and poverty. Japan was very successful in one respect, but was awful in the other aspect. As we observed in Chapters 5 and 6, to equate the growth of *GNP* (also applied to *GDP*) with that of economic welfare could be seriously questioned.

Since economic growth is measured in terms of *GNP* (*GDP*) growth, we explore the reasoning of this question. We deal with the weakness of the *GNP* concept based on the market-oriented economy and its improvement toward welfare-oriented society. First, we explain some weaknesses of the *GNP* concept: market failures in the measurement of *GNP*, distortions or limitations of the *GNP* concept viewed from the welfare point, and social imbalance. Then, we discuss the Net National Welfare (*NNW*) Index, which was established to cope with some of the drawbacks in the *GNP* concept. As a further development, we examine the Genuine Progress Indicator (*GPI*), social indicators, and happiness research. Finally, we propose an integrated idea for the welfare-oriented society, and we discuss some results and lessons from the bubble economy.

M. Iyoda, *Postwar Japanese Economy*, DOI 10.1007/978-1-4419-6332-1_9,
© Springer Science+Business Media, LLC 2010

9.1 Weaknesses of the *GNP* (Applied to *GDP*) Concept

9.1.1 Market Failures in the Measurement of GNP

Tsuru (1993, p. 141) explains the concept of *GNP* as that which "is predicated on the exchange of goods in the market, and is intended to cover these goods and services that are exchanged in the market." "As a corollary to this, it may be added that the unit of measurement of *GNP* is money value as registered in the market."

We examine market failures using the measurement of *GNP* from both theoretical and factual points. Tsuru examines this matter in brief as follows (Tsuru 1993, pp. 141–2). The measurement of *GNP* is based on the following three italicized assumptions; however, all are questionable. First, *external effects, either positive or negative, are unimportant*, whereas negative external effects such as pollution are often serious enough. Second, *the condition of consumer sovereignty is obtained*; however, (1) manufacturers often make the market and (2) we often observe the demonstration and dependent effects.[1] Third, *the failure of the reward system, for whatever reason, is of little inconsequence*, whereas the discriminating bias, particularly inheritance, provides great fortune to a select group of persons independently of their own efforts.

We may call these theoretical and factual failures in the measurement of *GNP*. If these market failures are considered significant, a longer-range association between the size of *GNP* and the magnitude of economic welfare can not be predicated.

9.1.2 Distortions or Limitations of the GNP Concept (from the Viewpoint of Welfare)

We now explain various market distortions of the *GNP* concept from the welfare viewpoint. First, the *GNP* unit of measurement is money value determined by the market. Therefore, nonmarket activities are excluded. Excluded examples are the quality of consumer goods (efficiency, durability, and so on), housekeeping work, and voluntary activities, and so on. These are very important from the viewpoint of welfare or of the quality of life. Business activities are profit-oriented, so that the product durability will not be their primal aim, for example. Unless the price of the goods increases, total annual sales in the long run will decrease as the goods' durability increases.

On the other hand, all market activities are included in *GNP*. *GNP* includes negative external effects (pollution), real estate transactions, and military products. Pollution is the negative from the welfare viewpoint. Real estate transactions increase *GNP*, but the transaction results only mean the change of owner. As a whole society, the welfare is not improved. Military products do not increase the welfare level.

Tsuru (1993, pp. 142–5) classifies four types as nonwelfare components of GNP, meaning that their welfare significance is questionable. Following is a brief summary of his explanation:

(1) "The cost of life" type. There are certain items that fall into the category of necessary costs, which we wish to remain as low as possible. Examples are heating costs in a cold climate, high commuting costs without compensating advantages in environmental amenities, and expensive burglar alarms to cope with the mounting incidence of burglary in homes.

(2) "The interference of income" type. Schumpeter originally used the term that might be defined as the generation of income by otherwise dispensable services, but which are made indispensable through built-in institutional arrangements in society. Examples are lawyers in the United States, bankers, real estate dealers, and tutoring schools for younger generations in Japan.

(3) "The institutionalization of waste" type. Waste is institutionalized in such a way that a less wasteful alternative, which may well be prepared by consumers, is deliberately withheld from the market. Vance Packard popularized the concept of built-in obsolescence in his writings, and the mechanism, which encourages this type of *GNP*-inflating expenditure, has been fully analyzed by Galbraith. Most notable examples during the high growth period of postwar Japan were the deliberate obsolescence of consumer durables such as cameras, refrigerators, and television sets, matched by the excessive advertising expenditures by producers and sellers.

(4) The depletion of social wealth. We can make our *GNP* even larger than otherwise would be the case by depleting our store of resources without replacing them. In this respect, the growth period of postwar Japan was a good example. Resource examples are earth's mineral deposits, forestry and marine resources, natural beauty, and other environmental endowments.

Our second point is that *GNP* is not a stock but a flow category, although imputed rent of dwellings and the depreciation of tangible infrastructures are included. The latter had not been considered until the current 93*SNA*. From the quality of life viewpoint, actual conditions of household asset holdings and living infrastructures are important. Third, *GNP* does not imply the degree of equality of income distribution and social security. We can examine part of income distribution and social security on a macro economy by using national income data, but the data are not sufficient for closer examination.

It is now clear that *GNP* itself does not represent the quality of life or the welfare level. To cope with these drawbacks, the *NNW Index* was developed. It is similar to the pioneering work, "Measure of Economic Welfare" (*MEW*), conducted by Nordhaus and Tobin (1971).

Finally, we refer to the fundamental question of the *GNP* concept that reflects the money value registered in the market. The market is predicated by the "money votes" of consumers where the rich and the poor are indifferent in terms of voting dollar rights. As a result, the composition of produced goods and services reflects what rich people consume. However, the marginal utility of income between the rich and the poor is greatly different, so that the market could be distorted. Suppose rich people spend a large amount of money on their pets or some extremely extravagant consumption, then a great amount of goods and services will be used up by these expenditures. This may have a significant negative effect on the satisfaction level for society as a whole.

9.2 Toward a Welfare Viewpoint

9.2.1 NNW *and the Questions*

To cope with distortions in the *GNP* concept from the welfare viewpoint, *NNW* was constructed by revising *GNP*. The idea is to subtract nonwelfare items (pollution, military expenditure, commuting time, and so on) from *GNP*, adding welfare-related items by monetary assessment (leisure time, housekeeping work, voluntary activities, and so on) to *GNP*. Services of most of the living infrastructures and durable consumer goods are added and the cost of legal system, police, fire defense, and general administration is deducted. This index signifies the welfare level better than that of *GNP*. See Nordhaus and Tobin (1971) and *NNW* Development Committee, National Council (1973), for details.

There are, however, some questions about *NNW*. First is value judgment. How can the welfare significance of any particular goods and services be determined? The values of some items are easy as they are determined by people. Second is how do we assess the value of nonmarket activities. The part-time hourly wage may apply to housekeeping work. But can the same wage rate be applied to leisure time and voluntary activities? These questions are not so easy to answer.

Third, there is not an effective demand for most assessed nonmarket activities because they are not really based on real financial transactions. The last point has a serious flaw, if we want to use this *NNW* concept for macroeconomic policy. For example, a stay-at-home spouse's work is the equivalent to 253,000 yen per month,[2] but she cannot buy anything with this assessed value.

9.2.2 NNW *and Some Estimates*

The *NNW* index is a step forward for measurement of welfare, but it is a weak tool for determining policy. *GNP* is still an important source for public policy decisions and *NNW* is useful for assessing economic results (performance) in terms of welfare. Therefore, these two indexes are complementary. (See *NNW* Development Committee, Economic Council 1973, p. 3 and Part 1; Iyoda 2006, pp. 27–8; Iyoda 2008.) We will discuss the importance of these two indexes in Section 9.4.

According to the *NNW* Development Committee, Economic Council (1973, p. 14), the ratio of *NNW* to *NDP* (excluding net investment) gradually decreased: 1.15 (1955), 1.07 (1960), 1.02 (1965), and 0.92 (1970) (fiscal year in parentheses). Figure 9.1 shows *NEW versus NNP*. *NEW* (Net Economic Welfare) is a similar type of index to the *NNW*. In the United States, per capita *NNP* (real) increased by a factor of 2 during the period from 1950 to the late 1980s; however, per capita *NEW*

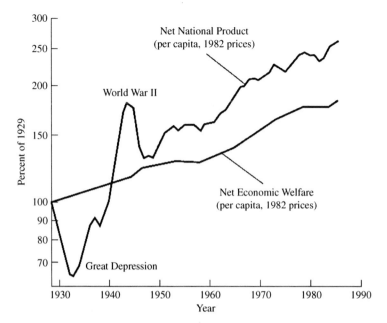

Fig. 9.1 Net economic welfare versus net national product
Source: Samuelson and Nordhaus, 1989, Fig. 6.3

increased only by a factor of 1.5. The gaps between these two per capita categories have become wider.

9.2.3 Social Imbalance

As we explained earlier (Chapter 6, Section 6.1), social balance between privately produced goods and services and those of the public sector is important. However, the inherent tendency that public services always fall behind private production causes social imbalance. This social imbalance is apt to be serious, particularly during the rapid economic growth period, causing and intensifying negative results or distortions in economic growth. In this regard, the market-oriented economy is ineffective in solving this problem. Even if the market mechanism works properly, the market itself cannot determine resource allocation between public services and private production to attain social balance.

Therefore, the question of social balance may lead to the question of public choice and the size of government. Some infrastructures, such as schools, hospitals, railways, communications, expressways, and housing, could be developed by the private sector, particularly in developed economies. This matter relates to the intrinsic question of the efficiency of resource allocation and justice. Actual policy is carried out according to the nation's choice.

Social imbalance results in social maladies. As long as public services lag, environmental disruption may become serious and the social welfare level will also fall behind production growth. If the government is strong enough to maintain social balance, these maladies can be avoided. As we examined in Chapters 2 and 5, Japanese income distribution greatly improved under the labor shortage in the 1960s, and social security (pension, medical insurance, and so on) greatly improved during the rapid growth period. However, environmental disruption became worse during the same period.

9.3 Further Development

NNW is a revised category of GNP, aiming at addressing the distortions in the GNP concept from the viewpoint of welfare. Therefore, this category still shares the remaining weaknesses with those of GNP. Further improvements along this line are the GPI (Genuine Progress Indicator) and the ISEW (Index of Sustainable Economic Growth). If we consider the measurement of total welfare, we need to consider a more general and broader aspect. In line with this, there has been more literature written about this during these past three decades. Further developments include social indicators and the measurement of happiness. We should note, however, that these applications indicate a further departure from a macroeconomic applicability of the national account category.

In the following section, we examine some of these important findings on the basis of which a high quality of life society is constructed.

9.3.1 The GPI

GPI (or the same sort of ISEW) is constructed by incorporating various aspects of economic wellbeing that are either ignored or treated incorrectly in GDP forecasts. Largely omitted are contributions of family and community, and the natural environment. The GPI "attempt[s] to undertake (1) welfare equivalent income, (2) sustainable income, and (3) net social profit" (Talberth et al. 2007, p. 3). The social cost of inequality, the diminishing returns to income received by the wealthy,[3] and the depletion of nature's endowments are now taken into consideration. Net social profit is a measure of policy effectiveness, indicating whether or not the proposed policy is welfare enhancing.

Figure 9.2 shows the per capita GPI and the per capita GDP in the United States (1950–2004). The per capita GDP was steadily increasing; however, the per capita GPI was growing until the mid-1970s, and then stagnating. The gaps between these indicators have been wider and wider since the mid-1970s. A similar example is observed in the United Kingdom (1950–1996) (see Jackson et al. 1997). For Australia (1950–2000), the per capita GPI is growing but very slowly (Hamilton 2003, Fig. 1 quoted from Hamilton and Dennis 2000). The gaps between these

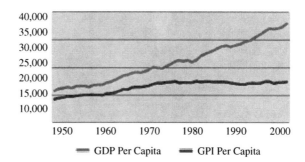

Fig. 9.2 Real GDP and GPI per capita 1950–2004 in $2000. *Source*: Talberth et al. (2007), Fig. 3

indicators have become ever wider. The figure may suggest what more important is in the society. We will not have a truly satisfied society unless we consider values other than growth of income.

9.3.2 Social Indicators

In the 1970s and 1980s, most *OECD* member nations grappled with developing social indicators that could measure the real quality of life that could not be valued in monetary terms. In Japan, the Economic Planning Agency developed and released social indicators from 1974 to 1985, and improved new social indicators from 1986 to 1991. Then, in 1992–1999, people's life indicators were introduced to quantify statistical indicators by dividing the activity field (dimension) into eight. Social indicators were also developed at the prefecture level in Japan. As of January 1985, 43 out of 47 prefecture governments used these indicators (Quality-of-Life Policy Bureau (QLPB) of EPA 1989, pp. 100–3), and used quality of life indicators 33 out of 47 prefectures as of February 1992 (QLPB of EPA 1992, pp. 224–5).

The social indicator approach seemed to be lacking a coherent, integrative conceptual framework to obtain the consensus. The movement has since waned. Statistical data of social indicators themselves are important, and since 1977, the Statistics Bureau (formerly SB of MCA and currently SB of MIAC) has annually published these statistics in prefectures in Japan.

9.3.3 Measurement of Happiness (Happiness Research)

The measurement of happiness has presented some important and intriguing findings. Reported subjective wellbeing seems to rise with income; however, once a threshold (*GNP* per capita in *ppp* 1995[4] around US $10,000) is reached, the average income level in a country has little effect on average subjective wellbeing. (See Frey and Stutzer 2002a, Figure 4 based on the data in 51 countries.) This suggests that for the quality of life satisfaction the threshold income of US $10,000 may be critical.

"The bigger income the better living satisfaction thinking" does not, however, mean a more satisfied society. (See also Frey and Stutzer 2002b[5])

Research for 49 countries in the 1980s and 1990s suggests that there are substantial wellbeing benefits from institutional factors. The data show that "the effects flowing directly from the quality of institutions are often much larger than those that flow through productivity and economic growth (Jhon Helliwell 2001)" (Frey and Stuzer 2002a, pp. 402–3). This means that institutional conditions such as the quality of governance and the size of social capital have important effects on an individual's wellbeing. See also Helliwell and Hung (2006) for their subsequent study on the government and wellbeing.

9.4 *GDP, GPI,* and Happiness Research

In this section, we pose the question of how a welfare-oriented society should be constructed. Our current society is a capitalist society based on private ownership of properties. The society heavily depends on a profit-oriented market. We explained that the *GDP* growth could not be a sign of welfare growth. The *GNP* concept had measurement failures and conceptual limitations from the welfare viewpoint. However, *GDP* is hardly replaced by *NNW*, which presents a weakness in monitoring economic activity and policy decisions, particularly economic stabilization policy. *NNW* is not an index based on effective demand. The government has measured the *GDP* every year, using it for policy judgment.

We showed examples (United States, Japan) that the gap between per capita *GNP* and *NEW* (or *NNW*) has become wider. The same was true of per capita *GDP* and *GPI*. Per capita *GPI* was decreasing or slowly growing since the mid-1970s in the United States, the United Kingdom, and Australia versus the steady growing per capita *GDP* since 1950. This is a serious concern. In addition, recent happiness research showed the threshold income of per capita *GDP* for the living satisfaction.

We mentioned that both categories of *GNP* and *NNW* are complementary, and both are needed for research. The real question is what weight or priority should be put on each category. Two findings mentioned above are important: *GPI* is decreasing or slowly growing since the mid-1970s; the threshold income is *GNP* per capita in *ppp* 1995 around US $10,000. The top priority should be given to the per capita *GPI* concept. Social and economic policy should be focused on the factors that may relate to *GPI*. Such factors include income distribution, market failures, environment, and social security. *GDP* growth is not a vital factor, for *GDP* growth is accompanied by the negative factors in *GPI*. The current *GDP* should be used for the practical purpose of judging economic conditions. The concrete policy should be based on whether or not the policy is *GPI* enhancing. The economic performance would be well assessed by *GPI*.

This standpoint is that economic growth expressed by *GDP* is not a necessary requisite to solving economic problems in the advanced countries; we do not use a maximization policy of economic growth by putting some constraints on the operation of market. It is true that the government can easily solve economic problems by making the pie larger during economic growth. Economic problems would be solved by the well-organized policy in advanced countries rather than by increasing per capita *GDP*.

For example, we observe poverty amid the affluent societies. The poverty rate in percentage terms (2000 and 2001 for Germany) was 17.1 (United States), 15.3 (Japan), 11.4 (United Kingdom), 10.0 (Germany), 7.0 (France), 5.3–6.4 (Scandinavian countries), and the *OECD* average (20) was 11.6 (Förster and Mira d'Ercole 2005). The rate depends on the definition but primarily reflects income distribution due to social and economic structures in the country. In the following two chapters, we deal with important factors that may relate to our ideal society: income and asset distribution, the relative share, household, and pension.

Viewed from the welfare point, the *GDP* concept has measurement failures and limitations. In this respect, *GPI* (further development of *NNW* and *NEW*) is an improved index. From the viewpoint of happiness, *GPI* is largely insufficient to fulfill demanding conditions. Happiness is a wider and more complicated concept, of which there is no easy integrated policy system. (See Frey and Stutzer 2002b.) Our idea here is to give top priority to *GPI*, which selects the government policy whether or not it is *GPI* enhancing. At the same time, important findings of happiness research should be taken into consideration. Examples are threshold income for the living satisfaction level and substantial wellbeing benefits from institutional factors.

Hamilton (2003) has a strong and decisive attitude about this problem. He recognizes, "capitalism has moved to a phase of abundance, and abundance broadly spread" (p. xv), but the society is still under growth fetish. He proposes "eudemonism" as an alternative political program. "The new, post-growth political philosophy of eudemonism proposes a society in which people can pursue the activities that truly can improve their individual and collective wellbeing. It is built on a consideration of the evidence for what does and does not contribute to a more contented society" (op. cit., p. xiv).

Our welfare-oriented society is not yet at the level of the societies of which Hamilton describes. Happiness would be the final and eternal purpose of human life. In this respect, we can share "eudemonism" with Hamilton. The practical policy would be different. Our above-mentioned goal would be more concrete and restricted, so that it may have a higher probability of being attained.

9.5 Some Lessons from the Bubble Economy

9.5.1 Overview

What have we learned from the bubble economy and its collapse and the prolonged depression that followed it? The Japanese industry was very successful in coping with the oil crisis. Japan's trade surplus enormously expanded from 1981 onward. To cope with the huge US trade deficit, under an agreement called the Plaza Accord, G5 agreed to further the dollar's decline. After this agreement, the Japanese yen greatly appreciated during the short period. This resulted in a serious blow to Japanese export industries and generated depression. The shock was so serious for these industries that the Bank of Japan reduced the official rate to the record low of 2.5 percent (until that time). This triggered an increase in loans for speculative trading in shares and real estate. To cope with recession, the government introduced a huge emergency spending package. Based on the result, some of these policies were unnecessary. Even in the high-yen recession, nonexport-oriented industries had strong growth. Reflecting the capital gains obtained from rising share prices and land appreciation, domestic demand was strong.

The Japanese exchange rate suffered from overreaction in the mid-1980s (after the Plaza Accord). Monetary and fiscal policies also overreacted to the yen's great appreciation after the Plaza Accord. This overreaction was partly caused by the serious situation that the export-oriented industries were facing, and partly by the fact that the policy makers failed to recognize that the economy lagged behind actual changes (economic data usually has a time lag). Stock and land prices were at abnormally high levels, which were not sustainable. As a result of gradual interest rate hikes from May 1989, stock prices fell sharply in early 1990, resulting in large capital losses. The Japan-US Structural Impediment Initial Talks (1989–1990) also affected the decline of stock prices; however, the decline in real estate prices lagged. The introduction of "real estate loan restrictions" by the Ministry of Finance stopped the land price increase and virtually halted it in 1992. *BIS* regulation affected the real estate declines. Then domestic demand cooled down and overcapacity in the manufacturing industry became apparent.

Japanese firms intensified attempts to export and the yen rate to the dollar sharply increased in late 1994. This situation intensified after the monetary and fiscal crisis brought about by *NAFTA,* which started with the Mexican crisis. The exchange rate registered at 79.75 yen in 1995, which caused serious difficulties for Japanese export industries and encouraged them to transfer their factories abroad, accelerating Japan's industrial hollowing out. The extremely low interest rate and the large government spending plans could not revive the Japanese economy until structural reform was strongly put into practice. The restructuring of corporations and the government deregulation policy contributed to the Japanese recovery.

Domestic economy is greatly affected in an unstable global economy. It is always difficult to expect moderate adjustment of fundamental disequilibrium in the world economy. Under these circumstances, the domestic economy is apt to suffer from a drastic change. The Japanese bubble economy and its consequence was an example. The bubble economy is a monetary phenomenon accelerated by the money game. Its context is profits-oriented capitalism, under which business enterprises seek higher profits. The origin of money, whether it is obtained as capital gains or corporate profits from business activities, is not questioned. Under this circumstance, fiscal and monetary policies are limited in preventing the generation of the bubble economy. However, if these policies are prudent and timely, the bubble-generating process may be slower and even slacken.

To summarize, first, based on the result, monetary and fiscal policies are responsible for generating the bubble economy. The policy authorities' overreactions to the yen's appreciation after the Plaza Accord caused and intensified the bubble economy. Second, the bubble economy is a monetary phenomenon accelerated by the money game, which cannot be avoided in a capitalist society. What we can do is to make the bubble generating process slower by making prudent and timely policies. Third, after the bubble collapsed, the Japanese economy had both huge bad loans and government bonds and debts. The economy suffered from prolonged stagnation and its recovery since 2002 was slow and weak. An important backdrop is that many economists and the policy authorities lacked sufficient recognition of the seriousness of "stock adjustments" and the Japanese economy greatly lagged behind globalization.

9.5.2 Some Lessons

First of all we should recognize the cost of the bubble during and after its collapse. During the bubble economy, we observed the following: (1) deterioration of asset and income distribution, in particular asset distribution; (2) large distortions of the resource allocation; and (3) serious housing problems. After the bubble burst, we had (1) huge nonperforming loans in Japanese banks, (2) outstanding government bonds, and (3) prolonged stagnation period.

As Soros (1998) mentions, global capitalism has intrinsic instability and the bubble economy could not be avoided. It is difficult to find the best possible solution to this matter. However, we suggest the following countermeasures as the second best.

First, overreactions must be avoided on the part of (1) policymakers, (2) business corporations, and (3) individuals. The government needs to supply fair information promptly and broadly. Once overconfidence or the loss of confidence takes hold, a moderate or calm attitude is difficult to achieve. Second, the bubble economy stems from soaring prices of shares, housing, land, and primary commodities from which companies and individuals intend to obtain capital gains. Therefore, a hedge environment and the futures markets should be prepared in advance of such a situation. Third, business ethics and the spirit of compliance should be fostered on a continuous basis. After the first oil crisis, the Japanese economy was so strong, until the bubble burst, that these ethics were quite weak, if not nonexistent. The capitalist society is based on the principle of self-responsibility.

Fourth, the international economy is largely directed by international capital under global capitalism. In order to stabilize the economy, international cooperation among the nations should be established. For this purpose, we have various international organizations such as *IMF*, *WTO*, World Bank, and *OECD*, which have had an important role in the development and stability of world economy. However, we need some ingenuity to complement the market imperfection under the current information technology. Finally, society learns more through painful rather than easygoing prosperous experiences. For example, compare the experiences after the first oil crisis with those after the bubble economy burst. As Itoh (2000) mentioned,

Japan's success brought "a series of setbacks to the Japanese economy in the 1990s" (p. 93) and the early 2000s until the recovery in 2002.

The Japanese bubble developed domestically although it was influenced by the international capital. Most lessons are domestically related, and we can take future countermeasures by learning these lessons, but the difficulty may be caused through the excessive "capital-gain seeking market behavior" in the profits-oriented capitalist background. Various ingenuities will relax or weaken the influence of the bubble. As Soros mentioned, the bubble economy could not be avoided and may have been guided by the avaricious nature of human beings. In this respect, government regulations and restrictions over the market would be effective to some extent, but may have limitation as lessons related to people and business reactions, business ethics, and the spirit of compliance are questions for the realms of psychology, morale, and philosophy. People's behavior depends on what kind of value they put on life. An important influencing factor may be education, which we will discuss in the last chapter.

The bubble economy was also influenced by the international market—unavoidable under the global capitalism. Returning to a closed economy is not an effective way for the development of a world economy. International cooperation is inevitable.

In conclusion, we consider lessons from the bubble economy from the viewpoint of welfare-oriented society. Above-mentioned costs of the bubble during and after the collapse all had deteriorating effects on a welfare society. Those costs were serious and extremely huge. From a whole society perspective, the bubble economy was not a zero-sum game but everyone lost. The bubble economy was not avoidable. And if faced again with this situation, we have two ways of dealing with it. First is to have creativity with policy controls and market regulations, which may relax or weaken the effect of the bubble. The other way is to set a safety net for the people who may have more difficulty sustaining their standard of living and become victims of economic fluctuations or disaster.

This viewpoint basically shares Rawls' *difference* principle (1971).[6] The principle states that social and economic inequalities are arranged so that they are to be the greatest benefit to the least-advantaged members of society. We live in an uncertain world and everyone has a possibility to become worse off.

We explained the process of the bubble economy's collapse, the consequences, and the reasons for the prolonged stagnation. Extremely high share and land prices were not sustainable, and share prices peaked in December 1989 and land prices in March 1990. In 1990, the decline in stock prices was large and the capital losses were huge. In 1991, the capital losses in real estate were added and the economy gradually went into depression. The Japanese firms again intensified attempts to export. As the trade surplus increased, the yen was appreciated greatly.

The greatly appreciated yen accelerated Japan's industrial "hollowing out." The tremendous decline in stock and real estate prices increased capital losses. As a result, nonperforming loans in the banks increased. In addition, a great earthquake hit the Kobe area in 1995, in which some 6400 people were killed. With the weak economy and increasing *NPLs*, the Asian financial crises erupted in July 1997. The great decline in stock prices sharply increased the bad debt burden of large banks and other financial institutions. Although government deployed huge amounts of public money in a rescue operation of banks and other financial institutions, Japan fell into the financial crisis.

Stagnation continued for about 10 years. Several explanations for this prolonged stagnation have been attempted. We considered two questions as important causes: "stock adjustments," and worldwide globalization connected with information technology.

Notes

1. The demonstration effect means that individual's behavior is affected by other consumer's behavior. The dependent effect is that the clever and eye-catching marketing strategy affects an individual's choice of goods and services and makes consumers purchase what they do not really need.
2. According to 1996 data by DNA of ERI, EPA (1998, Table 1), a full-time housewife's work, which was measured by the method of opportunity cost, was equivalent to an annual income of 3.04 million yen. By adding this total, the GDP increased 23.2 percent.
3. Welfare equivalent income is estimated from "personal consumption expenditures, which are weighted by an index of the inequality in the distribution of income to reflect the social costs of inequality and diminishing returns to income received by the wealthy" (loc. cit.).
4. The *ppp* (purchasing power parity) exchange rate is an exchange rate between two currencies such that the same basket of goods and services could be bought in each country, instead of indicated by market or the fixed rate.
5. Frey and Stuzter (2002b) is "the first book establishing the link between happiness and economics" and its originality is "to emphatically show that the more democratic and the more decentralized a country is, the happier people tend to be" (p. vii).
6. Rawls derived this idea by postulating that it is the principle that we should choose to live by, if we were asked to make a choice before finding out whether we ourselves were to be rich or poor. He proposes the two principles of justice for institutions. "(1) Each person is to have an equal right to the most extensive total system of equal basic liberties compatible with a similar system of liberty for all." "(2) Social and economic inequalities are to be arranged so that they are both: (a) to the greatest benefit of the least advantaged, consistent with the just savings principle, and (b) attached to offices and positions open to all under conditions of fair equality of opportunity" (1971, p. 302; 1999, p. 266). Rawls' second principle of justice gives the priority of justice over efficiency and welfare. He considers all social primary goods are to be distributed equally, which include rights, liberties and opportunity, income and wealth, and the basis of self-respect. (see Gotok 2002 for the study of Rawls' *Theory of Justice*.)

h

Chapter 10
Income and Asset Distribution, and the Relative Share

This chapter and the next chapter deal with some of the important economic issues in relation to a welfare-oriented society. These are income and asset distribution, the relative share of income, household structure, and pension. We examine the first two issues in this chapter. Among others, income and asset distribution is an important economic issue that has been under heated discussion in both the academic and political worlds of Japan, in particular in the 2000s.

After the bubble burst in the early 1990s, the Japanese economy stagnated for about 10 years and the unemployment rate largely increased from 2 percent to a level exceeding 5 percent. In addition, the Japanese population is aging. Income distribution has become a more serious economic issue under these economic conditions.

Income distribution is broadly divided into two fields. One is personal distribution, which is the share-out of national income between various factor input suppliers and recipients. We usually discuss the question of income equity or disparity. The other is functional distribution, which is the share-out of national income between various factor inputs. This ordinarily leads to the question of the relative share of income.

10.1 Income Distribution

10.1.1 Inverse U-Shaped Hypothesis

Simon Kuznets (1955) presented the "inverse U-shaped hypothesis" describing the relationship between income distribution and economic growth, and verified this hypothesis by surveying 18 advanced countries in 1963. The hypothesis is that in the beginning stage of economic growth, income distribution worsens, and then it gradually reverses and goes in a better direction.

It can be explained as follows: In the beginning stage of economic growth, a large income differential sector expands rapidly, which is a nonagricultural sector. The income differential is relatively small in the agricultural sector. As a result, income distribution worsens. As the weight of the nonagricultural sector becomes large, the effect of income differentials between the two sectors on the total income distribution becomes smaller. We observe the property income reduction in a relative sense, and the promotion of both social security and full employment. Reflecting these, income distribution gradually proceeds to equalization.

10.1.2 Japanese Case

What changes we have seen in income distribution after World War II? Figure 2.4 in Chapter 2 shows two kinds of Gini coefficients of income distribution in Japan. We classify Japanese income distribution into four periods:

> 1950–1960 worsening
> 1961–1969 rapid equalization
> 1970–1979 staying at the same level and slightly worsening
> 1980– worsening

Figure 2.4 observes the trends since 1961. For 1950–1960, Figures (2.5, 2.6a, 2.6b) show the sharp contraction of the primary industry in terms of production and labor force. However, there does not seem to be a definite estimate that shows deterioration of income distribution throughout these years. We have various data that show the expansion of wage differentials between the company sizes: white- and blue-collar workers, men and women, and age brackets in the 1950s. Gini coefficients of the workers' and the nonagricultural households peaked in 1961, the former of which showed slightly increasing signs from 1955 (see p. 25 n4 for the meaning of Gini coefficient). We consider that income distribution deteriorated during the period of 1950–1960. (see Iyoda 1991, Ishizaki 1983.)

Does Kuznets' hypothesis mentioned above apply to the Japanese economy? One argument is for what time span we should consider the hypothesis. If we apply his hypothesis to the postwar period, it seems to be true.[1] After equalization process, however, income distribution has been deteriorating, particularly since the 1980s. Since the 1990s, there have been attempts to explain the reason behind this worsening process.

The aging Japanese population (the demographic change) may explain the worsening trend. Gini coefficients by age bracket in Japan become higher as the age goes up. As the age goes up, the wage differentials go up between both the white-collar and the manual workers, and the manager and the non-manager groups. Furthermore, after the retirement age, the income differences among the retired, the non-retired, and the self-employed become greater. In this context, the shift of the baby boom generation (born in 1946–1948) explains the major cause of worsening of Japanese income distribution. Since the 1980s in Japan, the demographic change explains the major change of the Gini coefficient.

Ohtake (2005, Chapter 1) demonstrated that (1) income distribution within the age bracket was stable, and (2) the difference of income distribution by age bracket was greater as the age goes up during the period from 1979 to 1999. This suggested that the income disparity was caused by the aging factor. (See Ohtake 1994 for this idea of the income disparity in the 1980s.) His estimate was based on households with two and more members based on *National Survey of Family Income and Expenditure* (SB of MIAC (e) (ed.)). He also quotes from *Income Redistribution Survey* (Survey Section of PDMS, MHLW (ed.)) which explains about 64 percent of the income deterioration (before tax, between 1999 and 2002) is a result of the aging factor and 25 percent by the decrease of family size. Note that this survey includes one-person households. Ohtake mentions that the influence of aging factor over income distribution depends on the data and the period taken for the estimate. "The income disparity caused by the demographic change is not a true deterioration" (Ohtake 1994, p. 22).

Income distribution has become not only an economic but a political issue in Japan, particularly since the early 2000s. There has been heated discussion regarding the cause of income distribution deterioration, and on where the Japanese income distribution ranks in international comparison.

The greatest mission of the Koizumi administration, which began in April 2001, was "to end the slump in the Japanese economy that was known as 'the lost decade.' Moreover, to that end, Koizumi announced that he would implement policies that were vastly different from those of previous administrations, that is, the so-called 'structural reforms'" (Takenaka 2008, p. ii).[2] He explicitly proposed privatization or abolition of special corporations and reduction of local allocation tax. Such examples included privatization of the postal system and the Japan Highway Public Corporation, the reform of Zaisei Toyushi, and broad-ranging regulatory reforms. As Japan was facing a rapidly aging society, he intended to form a small government with urgent priority.

It has been questioned whether the recent deterioration was caused by Mr. Junichiro Koizumi's "structural reforms." One well-known fact is that income distribution has been deteriorating in the United States, the UK, and Japan since the 1980s. These three countries have essentially taken the same economic policy, including the privatization of public corporations, the easing of regulation, and tax reforms. Therefore, we cannot deny that these factors have affected income distribution. For Japan, however, the demographic change has affected the income disparity, particularly since the 1980s.

10.1.3 International Comparison

International comparison of income distribution is difficult, and the resulting estimates depend on the data. The statistical data are not always collected in the same way among the countries. It will be necessary to interpret the results with some caution.

By using *OECD* data,[3] CAO of GoJ (2007) estimates the (equivalence based) Gini coefficient of the member countries based on the household disposable income. The Japanese coefficient is slightly higher than that of the average of

OECD members, which ranks among the lowest of the middle-upper-ranking group including the UK and the United States (Fig. 3-3-10, p. 315).

The poverty index is another concept, which is used internationally to make comparisons of the income disparity. Förster and Mira d'Ercole (2005) show that Japan ranks as the fifth worst at 15.3 percent among *OECD* members regarding the relative poverty indicator. *OECD* defines the relative poverty as a proportion of people that do not satisfy the 50 percent median of income distribution. CAO of GoJ (2007) argues that the *OECD* analysis of Japan is based on *Comprehensive Survey of Living Condition of the People on Health and Welfare* (*SID*, Minister's Secretariat, MHLW (ed.), 2000 survey). However, if the same poverty rate is calculated based on *National Survey of Family Income and Expenditure*[4] (all households, 1999 survey), the rate is about 9 percent (Fig. 3-3-11, p. 317), which suggests a deviation. The *OECD*-based survey includes money remittance-receiving people such as students living alone. As a result, in terms of income distribution, a relatively larger number of households earning less than 2 million yen in the survey samples are included. As the result varies with the statistical data used, it is necessary to interpret the estimate results with some caution. For further argument, see Tachibanaki and Urakawa (2006) for a comprehensive survey of Japanese poverty.

10.2 Asset Distribution

10.2.1 Financial and Physical Assets

Figure 10.1 shows financial and land assets distribution. Observing this figure, the Gini coefficient of land assets was greater than that of financial assets, the latter of which seemed to be declining. For financial assets on one hand, there was an equalizing trend of the distribution from the early 1960s on, except for the bubble period, particularly for 1987–1989. On the other hand, the Gini coefficient of land assets jumped during the bubble years, then gradually decreased until 2000.

There are two kinds of difficulties in determining physical assets: (1) the lack of asset data in the long term and (2) problematic macroeconomic aggregation. Therefore, it is difficult to determine a long-term trend. Gini coefficients by area should be compared. Physical assets include both land and house (building), but in Fig. 10.1, we use only land assets.

10.2.2 Some Properties of Asset Distribution

There are some properties concerning asset distribution. First, there is positive correlation between income and home ownership; however, we found the J-shape relationship an exception. J-shape relationship means that a large number of pensioners rank in the lower income group, but their house ownership rate is high, so that their holding asset values are large. Average asset values of the first fifth income

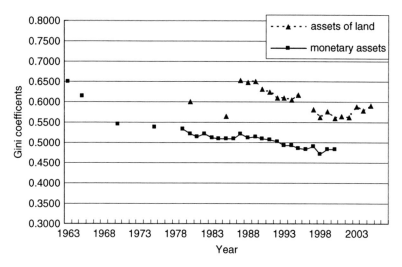

Fig. 10.1 Asset distribution.
Sources: CAO (2007), resources, 2(2); EPA of GoJ (c) (1994), Fig. II-1-36
Notes: Gini coefficients of the land asset are calculated on the site value of owned houses: based on the panel data of *Family Income and Expenditure Survey* (SB of MCA ed. and SB of MIAC ed.) and *Official Posting of Land Price* (Ministry of Land, Infrastructure, and Transport ed.). Gini coefficients of financial assets are of all households (nonagricultural households) based on *Family Savings Survey* (SB of MCA ed.)

group (the lowest 20 percent) are higher than the second fifth income group (the second lowest 20 percent). From the second fifth income onward, there is positive correlation between income and home ownership. We observed the J-shape relationship in the holding asset value and income space. (see Planning Bureau of EPA 1975, I, Chapter 3.)

Since 2000, the relationship became volatile. Observing yearly income deciles, the higher house ownership rate was shifting from the first to the second or the third deciles in the 1990s and the first half 2000s. This shift reflected average high yearly income of the aged, but they were divided into the lower and the higher income groups. Table 10.1 shows income, savings, and house ownership rates held per household by age group of head. Average yearly income for 60–69 years was 585 (unit, in 10,000 yen), which was in the sixth decile (average income, 589), and for 70 years and older was 466, which was in the fourth decile (average income, 442), in all households. (see SB of MIAC (c) 2007, Table 6; also Table 11.3 in Chapter 11.)

Second are bequests. It is estimated that about 40 percent of the household asset value stems from bequests; 40 percent is a large amount, which means the discriminating bias of the reward system. Inheritance is the property left by a deceased person and is not earned by individual effort. There are some difficulties in determining the inherited amount of assets. There is a theoretical question of how to impute the present value of assets between bequests and the legatee's contribution. The timing of bequests can have a tremendous effect on the estimate value.

Table 10.1 Income, savings, and house ownership rate by age group of household head (2007)

Household items	Household head by age group						
	Average	~29	30~39	40~49	50~59	60~69	70 and over
Yearly income (10,000 yen)	649	476	589	763	836	585	466
Savings (10,000 yen)	1,719	255	648	1,118	1,697	2,474	2,426
House ownership rate (%)	80.5	30.5	53.4	77.2	87.3	90.6	91.5

Source: SB of MIAC (c) (2007), Table 8

Tachibanaki and Takata (1994), Tachibanaki (1998, Chapter 4) explain the properties of the Japanese bequest. (1) Japanese household assets consist of more than 80 percent physical assets and the remaining financial assets; (2) 52.6 percent of physical assets were inherited in terms of present value, but the value of inherited financial assets was only 4.7 percent. About 44.5 percent of household assets were inherited; (3) physical assets contributed to some 30 percent deterioration of asset distribution, but the influence of financial assets was negligible.

Ohtake (2005) examines some findings of Horioka et al. (2002) that the average present value of inherited assets was 42 million yen, which accounted for 24 percent of total assets (based on 1996 survey data). He uses Takayama and Arita (1996)'s estimate that the inherited asset ratio was 33 percent based on 1992 survey data. The estimate greatly depends on data and the years surveyed.

Finally, we have an interesting observation about the income and asset distribution. Since the 1980s, the Japanese income distribution has been deteriorating; however, financial asset distribution since the 1960s had an equalizing trend until 2000, and since the bubble burst, land asset distribution experienced the same equalizing trend until the early 2000s. Financial asset distribution reflected the equalized (1960s) and the stagnated (1970s) income distribution, because financial assets of households are primarily accumulated savings from their yearly income. After the bubble collapsed, financial asset distribution probably reflected the declining and then stagnated stock prices to some extent. The decline of land prices might also relate indirectly to this distribution to a lesser extent. Although valid, these explanations are not enough to explain the equalizing trend of financial asset distribution since the 1980s. If the major cause of the Japanese income disparity was in the demographic change, the trend since the 1980s will not be a true deterioration. This may be an important underlying fact throughout this period.

10.3   Relative Share of Income

10.3.1   Estimates

We have alternative approaches (data) for the estimate of the relative share of income. One way is based on *National Accounts* where the labor share is calculated as

[Labor Income/National Income (*NI*)] or [Labor Income/Gross National Product (*GNP*)].

Another way is based on *Financial Statistics of Corporations* (PRI of MoF) where it is calculated as

[Personnel Costs/(Personnel Costs + Depreciation + Business Profits)].

This approach is useful for the estimate by industry (manufacturing, nonmanufacturing, and all aggregates) or by size of the corporation (all, large, and small and medium aggregates). However, the *Financial Statistics of Corporations* excludes self-employed businesses and the financial and the insurance industries. For quarterly data, small corporations with a capital less than 10 million yen are excluded. Both financial and insurance industries have been included from FY 2008 survey.

Let us observe some of these estimates. Figure 10.2 shows the first approach with four kinds. The first group is estimates with imputation of the self-employed income between wages and profits using the asset and the labor bases; namely

[Employee's Compensation (Emp. C) + Imputed Wages)/*GNP*].

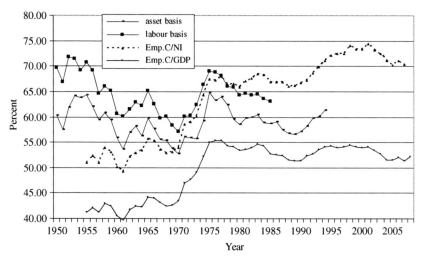

Fig. 10.2 Relative share of labor based on national income (1950–2008).
Sources: Iyoda (1987), Tables 1 and 2. CAO of GoJ (2009, Japanese ed.), Long-term economic statistics (nominal values) obtained from www5.cao.go.jp/wp/wp-je09/09p00000.html
Notes: 1 Relative share of labor (asset and labor bases) is measured as [(Employee's Compensation (Emp. C) +Imputed Wages)/*GNP*]. All values are in nominal terms, then *GNP* = *GNI* (Gross National Income) in this case; 2 Asset basis: The self-employed income is imputed by the assumption that the profit rate of the unincorporated enterprise is equal to that of incorporated enterprise; 3 Labor basis: the self-employed income is imputed by the assumption that average employee's income is equal to the weighted self-employed income (weighted by the average number of family workers); 4 The asset basis estimate is revised by making the capital gain adjustment since 1970

The second group is without imputation, being simply estimated as

[Emp. C/*NI*] *and* [Emp. C/*GDP*].

Estimates in each group are largely parallel. However, a significant difference between the groups is observed until the mid-1970s related to whether self-employed businesses are included.

If the self-employed businesses are not large and/or their share of the whole economy is stable, the imputation question may not occur. If they are as large as that in Japan some 60 years ago or in developing countries, we need to impute the self-employed income (mixed income) between wages and profits. For example, the self-employed income was some 43 percent of net national product (*NNP*) in 1952, and the labor force employed in the sector as the self-employed and family workers were some 60 percent in 1950. These high percentages have rapidly contracted, particularly during the rapid economic growth period. (see Chapter 2, Fig. 2.6b; Iyoda 1984, Tables 2 and 3.)

Figures 10.3 and 10.4 show the second approach mentioned above. Figure 10.3 shows the estimate of the labor share by industry. The relative share of labor varies from industry to industry, among which the manufacturing is lower than the non-manufacturing industries. These gaps may reflect the difference of productivity growth among the industries, which were large until 1985 (except for 1975) and for recent years 2004–2007. Figure 10.4 shows estimates by corporation size (all, large, and Emp. C for reference). The labor share of large corporations with a capital of one billion yen or more is low compared with all corporations' share, showing similar movements to the Emp. C/*GDP*. We do not show the estimate of small and medium corporations (due to a lack of annual data), but we can infer their high labor

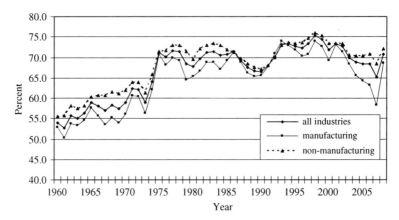

Fig. 10.3 Relative share of labor by industry (1960–2008).
Source: PRI of MoF (2009), annual data (fiscal year, without seasonal adjustments)
Note: The labor share = personnel costs/(personnel costs + depreciation + business profits)

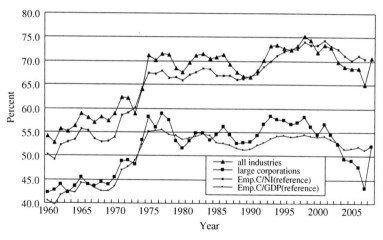

Fig. 10.4 Relative share of labor by size of corporation (1960–2008).
Sources: Same as in Figs. 10.2 and 10.3
Notes: 1 The labor share of all industries (all corporations) is a reproduction in Fig. 10.3; 2 Large corporations mean with a capital of one billion yen or more; 3 Emp. C/*NI* is the same as that in Figure 10.2

share through these two estimates of all and large corporations. We have quarterly data for small and medium corporations but not the same coverage of annual data. The labor share of all corporations is the reproduction of all industries in Fig. 10.3, which is close to the Emp. C/*NI*.[5]

10.3.2 Properties of the Relative Share of Labor

The labor share is a relative category, so that it cannot go to both extremes. The share fluctuates with relatively low and high periods that reflect various economic conditions. (see Iyoda 1987 for Japan and 1997, Chapter 2; Nishizaki and Sugou 2001 for cyclical movements.) The Japanese relative share of labor has the following properties: First, the labor share moves countercyclically, decreasing during the expansion period and increasing during the recession period. Second, it is generally low during the period of rapid economic growth and high during the slow economic growth period. Third, the relative share of labor by industry varies from industry to industry, and that by size of corporations varies from corporation size to corporation size.

Employed people may demand higher wages, although it may be a low labor share period. On the other hand, entrepreneurs may demand more profits while in the high labor share period. Can the relative share of income be directly a strategic policy variable? We deal with this question later. Before dealing with this question, however, we present a macroeconomic explanation of the relative share fluctuation (see Iyoda 1997, p. 28).

10.3.3 Macroeconomic Explanation

The relative share of labor (ρ_l) is defined as

$$\rho_1 = W/Y = w/e\mu \tag{1}$$

where W = wages, Y = output, w = money wages, e = price level, and μ = labor productivity. From equation (1), we have

$$\hat{\rho}_l = \hat{w} - (\hat{e} + \hat{\mu}) \tag{2}$$

where $\hat{\rho}_l = \dot{\rho}_l/\rho_l$, $\dot{\rho}_l = d\rho_l/dt$, and t = time period.

(a) Expansion period. Wages, price, and productivity generally increase during the expansion period. The growth rates of price ($\hat{e}$) and productivity ($\hat{\mu}$), however, will be higher than that of wages ($\hat{w}$). Hence, we have

$$\hat{w} < \hat{e} + \hat{\mu}, \text{so that } \hat{\rho}_l < 0.$$

The labor share will decrease. Technology progress and the operation-rate increase may bring relatively high productivity growth. Wage increases are apt to be behind the growth of price and productivity ($\hat{e} + \hat{\mu}$).

(b) Recession period. During the recession period, the process will be in contrast to the expansion period. The price increase is normally weak. Productivity will not increase much due to slow technology improvement and the lowered operation rate. However, wages are relatively sticky on the other hand. As a result,

$$\hat{w} > \hat{e} + \hat{\mu}, \text{so that } \hat{\rho}_l > 0.$$

Due to these reasons, we consider the labor share will fluctuate countercyclically. During the expansion period, the low labor share will be a result of good business conditions and vice versa during the recession period. The level of labor share can be a major factor in the wage bargaining between the labor union and the management, particularly during the expansion period. However, the government will have difficulty dealing with this factor as a strategic policy variable.

10.3.4 Remaining Questions

Under the low growth rate economy and the rapid aging society, income distribution has become an increasingly important economic issue. For the practical policy, recognizing the actual conditions of income distribution is a prerequisite condition. We argued that we have not had a systematic policy influencing functional distribution, although it is acknowledged that some policies bring full employment and keep prices stable and that some industrial policies will support these policies. [6]

There are two types of policies affecting personal distribution. The first type is a so-called income redistribution policy that is carried out through the taxation system and social security. The general aim of such a policy is to achieve a more equitable distribution of income to various sections of the community to ensure that everybody is provided with a minimum standard of living. The decision to enact these policies is actually decided politically. The second policy equalizes income sources, which is carried out through equal asset holding, equal educational opportunities, and equal opportunity in employment. Income redistribution has a large literature theoretically and empirically. Statistical tools and evaluation methods have been developed for such a policy. Equalization of holding income sources or their acquisition will be increasingly demanded by a society seeking high-level satisfaction.

This chapter dealt with income and asset distribution, and the relative share of income. We reviewed the postwar Japanese income distribution. The aging factor (the demographic change) mostly explained the deterioration of income distribution since the 1980s. In this respect, the Japanese income disparity was not a true deterioration. International comparison of income distribution is difficult, as estimate results differ according the data used. According to the Cabinet Office, Japan is among the lowest of the middle-upper-ranking group, including the UK and the United States.

We also looked at asset distribution. For the financial assets, there was an equalizing trend of distribution from the early 1960s onward, except for the bubble years, and particularly those for 1987–1989. Physical assets have data problems such as a lack of long-term time series data and macroeconomic aggregation. Gini coefficients of land assets jumped during the bubble years; however, since the bubble burst, they gradually declined until 2000.

Third, we explained that the relative share of income had two approaches in accordance with the data used. Estimates are restricted by the data coverage. The common features were countercyclical movements of the labor share, for which we gave a macroeconomic explanation. The labor share was generally low during the high growth period and *vice versa* for the low growth period. Finally, we referred to the policy relevance of income and asset distribution, and the relative share of income.

Notes

1. Takayama (1980) argues, "If we include capital gains in households income, the postwar economic growth of Japan does not always bring income equality" (p. 56). He asserts that Kuznets' hypothesis needs reexamination.
2. These reforms were against LDP's policy until then. Takenaka also mentioned that "Industries and companies with vested interests developed powerful connections with politicians, and then further collusion between such politicians and some bureaucrats meant that any progress at all in the socioeconomic reform of Japan seemed even more unlikely." (loc. cit.) Professor Heizo Takenaka (Keio University) was appointed the Minister for Economic and Fiscal Policy, where

he chaired the Council on Economic and Fiscal Policy and steered macroeconomic policy. In the following 5-1/2 years, he spearheaded Japan's economic structural reform.

3. Japanese figures are based on 2000 values and the other countries on 1999–2002 values except for the 1995 values of two countries.

4. Former survey is edited by Statistics and Information Department, Minister's Secretariat, MHLW, and SB of MIAC edits the latter. See data sources.

5. The data coverage will explain the similarity and the difference between the labor share of all corporations (all industries) and the Emp. C/NI. Both estimates exclude the self-employed businesses, and the former estimate furthermore excluded the financial and the insurance industries until 2007, but the latter estimate includes these. The two estimates showed an increasing trend until recently. We consider this a reflection of the continuous contraction of the self-employed businesses and an expansion of employee's compensation (due to both increases in the number of employees and their wages and salaries).

6. Financial and monetary policies aim at full employment, price stability, and efficiency of resource allocation in a broad sense. Other related policies are industrial policies that promote competition and protect or support particular industries. See Planning Bureau of EPA (Japan) (1975, pp. 105–7) for a discussion relating to this.

Chapter 11
Households and Pension

This chapter deals with two economic issues. First, we examine Japan's household structure. In the previous chapter (Chapter 10), we recognized the importance of the effect of the demographic change on the Japanese income distribution. Demographic changes are closely related to the pension issue. In dealing with the current and future economy and society, the household study is one of the important factors. Second, we discuss the pension issue, which has also provided heated discussion among the economic and political worlds.

11.1 The Japanese Households: Data

11.1.1 Data

We mostly depend on the following surveys on households in this chapter: *Family Savings Survey (FSS)* and the continued survey with revision, *Family Income and Expenditure Survey (FIES) <Savings and Liabilities>*. What are the criteria of these surveys? In interpreting the survey results, we should consider their properties.

FSS had been carried out since 1959, but this survey was integrated into *FIES* with revision in 2002, and published separately as a *Savings and Liabilities* division. The reason was that clarification of the actual conditions of the family income and expenditure in correlation with the status of holding savings and liabilities had become increasingly important. Data have no continuity to the former series of data in a strict sense. However, *FSS* is still used to overview the structural change of Japanese households. We should note the following properties beforehand for the interpretation of survey results.

The merits are as follows: (1) yearly quintile income data are available since 1959, and (2) the collected data correspond with the actual survey period. On the other hand, there are some weaknesses: (1) The number of survey samples (currently about 8,000; formerly less than this number) is relatively small compared with other surveys. (2) The survey deals with two and more member households,[1] and until 2000, agriculture households were excluded. The survey is based on bookkeeping,

M. Iyoda, *Postwar Japanese Economy*, DOI 10.1007/978-1-4419-6332-1_11,
© Springer Science+Business Media, LLC 2010

Table 11.1 One-person households

Item	2002	2007
Ratio to total number of households (%)	27.5	28.2
Earner per household	0.61	0.56
Age of head	51.7	55.0
of which 60 years and over (%)[a]	40.5	47.3
(65 years and over)	(34.0)	(40.5)
Yearly income (in 10,000 yen)	336	323
House ownership rate (%)	41.5	49.1
Engel's coefficient	23.3	22.5

[a] Adjusted number of tabulated households
Sources: SB of MIAC (b) (2002), One-Person Households (Table 2) and Total Households (Table 3); (2007), One-Person Households (Tables 1.1 and 2) and Total Households (Table 12)

so that the extremely rich and low-income households are excluded. Therefore, the survey largely covers the middle-income group and is biased to the relatively high-income groups. (see Iyoda 1991, pp. 26–7; Planning Bureau of EPA 1975, Tables I-1-1 and I-1-2.) Table 11.1 shows properties of one-person households.

11.2 The Structure of the Japanese Household

11.2.1 Structural Changes

Table 11.2 shows structural changes of the Japanese household. We observe various properties of the household: annual income, number of family members, number of persons working, savings, liabilities, dwelling owning rate, propensity to consume, age of household head, and so on, all of which are expressed on the average.

During the observation period, first, the family size continuously decreased from 4.46 (1960) to 3.18 persons (2005). The age of household head increased, particularly from about 1980 (45.4 years) to 2005 (54.7 years). Second, yearly income greatly increased until 1995 (7,620 thousand yen). Reflecting this, family savings greatly increased to 17,280 thousand yen (2005), and as a result, the saving ratio to yearly income largely increased to 267.9 percent (2005). The majority of financial assets held by households are demand and time deposits, exceeding half of the total except for the 1960s and the bubble years. Next is insurance, and so on, which is between 23.1 and 30.9 percent during the observation period. Third, securities decreased to a small percentage, although there was an upsurge during the bubble years. The Japanese household attitude is not profitability oriented but safety oriented. Japanese people prefer safe assets to risky assets.

Fourth, all values are averaged and thus can be misleading. In 2007, for example, average savings per household exceeded 17 million yen, but 67.8 percent of households had less average savings, and the largest group (14.8 percent) held less than

Table 11.2 Structural changes of the Japanese household[a] (1960–2005)

Year	1960	1965	1970	1975	1980	1985	1990	1995	2000	2005
Persons per household[b]	4.46	4.29	4.00	3.90	3.83	3.76	3.57	3.39	3.26	3.18
Earners per household[b]		1.63	1.60	1.56	1.53	1.55	1.52	1.55	1.47	1.42
Age of household head[b]	44.0	44.9	44.7	44.8	45.4	48.0	50.0	51.7	53.4	54.7
Yearly income[c]	45	78	139	299	464	556	677	762	721	645
Savings[c]	36	76	160	317	579	853	1,353	1,604	1,781	1,728
of which (%)										
deposits	45.7	46.2	51.4	59.3	59.9	54.7	49.5	55.9	58.4	59.3
insurance, etc.[d]	24.0	27.4	27.4	24.0	23.1	25.7	27.2	30.8	30.9	27.5
securities	30.4	26.4	21.1	16.7	17.1	19.6	23.3	13.1	10.7	13.1
Liabilities[c]	7	13	28	85	177	272	359	460	538	501
To yearly income (%)										
Savings ratio	79.2	97.4	115.0	106.0	124.8	153.5	199.8	210.5	246.9	267.9
Liabilities ratio	15.2	16.7	20.4	28.4	38.2	49.0	53.0	60.4	74.6	77.7
House owning ratio (%)				64.1	67.3	71.8	73.4	71.6	75.6	77.9
Engel's coefficient[e] (%)	38.7*	38.1	34.1	32.0	29.0	27.0	25.4	23.7	23.3	22.7
Propensity to consume[f]		82.8	79.7	77.0	77.9	77.5	75.3	72.5	72.1	74.7

[a]All (nonagricultural) households with two or more members, except for 2005 that includes agricultural households; Engel's coefficient and propensity to consume are values on workers' households. [b]The number of persons. [c]In 10,000 yen. [d]Including savings in nonfinancial institutions. [e]Engel's coefficient = food expense/living expenditure. The coefficient with asterisk is in 1963. [f]Propensity to consume (%) = living expenditure/disposable income

Sources: Japan Statistical Association (2006), Vol. 4, 20-11-b for all households except for house owning ratio; 20-2-c for workers' households. SB of MIAC(c) (2005) for workers' households for 2005. SB of MCA (d) (1988)

Notes: Data are based on *FSS* for 1960–2000 and *FIES*<Savings and Liabilities> for 2005. *FSS* was integrated to *FIES* with the revision of survey method in 2002. Therefore, since 2002, there is no continuity to the former data

2 million yen. A median was 10.18 million yen. There was a huge difference among households. (see SB of MIAC (c) 2007, Fig. 1.) For this reason we need to examine the household structure by dividing the quintile income and quintile savings groups.

11.2.2 Current Household Structure

Table 11.3 shows the household structure of Japan by quintile group for both yearly income and amount of savings. We observe several interesting properties of the Japanese household with two or more persons. First is the difference between all households and workers' households. All households include not only workers but also the self-employed and retired people, of which workers' households account for 55.3 percent (2007). The self-employed and the retired are relatively low-income groups. This explains the difference of values between the all households and the workers' households.

Second, the highest fifth group has the highest income, which reflects the high age of the working household head and large numbers of dual income (both man and woman working) households. (see the average number of earners per household and the average age of household head.)

Third, savings increase as yearly income grows; however, the saving ratio to yearly income is in reverse relative to yearly income. This may be partly caused by the aged (retired) people in the first and the second income quintile groups who have relatively huge amount of savings. (see yearly income and savings of household head by age group in Table 10.1.) Savings by yearly income quintile group suggest that the amount of savings of the majority households is below the average. We can also confirm the safety-oriented attitude of Japanese households in the composition of savings by quintile group of yearly income.

Engel's coefficients and propensity to consume are values on workers' households (with two or more persons). Engel's coefficients decrease as the theory and experiences suggest. The propensity to consume seems to depict a J-shape curve against savings. The lowest savings group of households has high propensity to consume because of the low income. The middle-savings group has a relatively heavy burden of their mortgage payments for houses, and land and property purchases. As a result, the propensity to consume by the lower middle-savings group may be lower than the lowest savings quintile.

Although Engel's coefficient of the highest savings group by quintile is the lowest, they have the highest propensity to consume. This is different from the result by yearly income quintile group, which is perhaps partly caused by the relatively large number of aged households in this quintile. The largest-saving households in workers' households were the age group of 60–69 in 2007. Their propensity to consume in percentage was fairly high at 89.2, although their sample distribution was 12.6 percent. Note that they broke into their savings both in 2005 and 2006. (see SB of MIAC (c) 2007, Tables 3 and 8; SB of MIAC (b) 2007, Two or More Persons Households, Table 2.) This may need further analysis.

Table 11.3 Household[a] structure of Japan (2007)

Item	All households (average)	of which (Yearly income quintile group)					(Reference) Workers' households
		I ~350[c]	II 350~476	III 476~634	IV 634~881	V 881~	
Persons per household[b]	3.15	2.59	2.84	3.25	3.45	3.62	3.46
Earners per household[b]	1.39	0.80	1.02	1.44	1.69	1.98	1.66
Age of household head[b]	55.5	62.1	58.0	52.4	51.2	53.7	47.2
Yearly income[c]	649	272	411	549	746	1,268	718
Savings[c]	1,719	1,227	1,589	1,585	1,645	2,550	1,268
of which (%)							
deposits	58.1	66.6	61.8	58.8	55.9	52.7	55.4
insurance, etc.[d]	26.3	21.5	21.6	26.8	30.0	28.8	32.5
securities	15.6	11.8	16.6	14.4	14.1	18.5	12.1
Liabilities[c]	505	149	272	475	681	947	664
To yearly income (%)							
Savings ratio	264.9	451.1	386.6	288.7	220.5	201.1	176.6
Liabilities ratio	77.8	54.8	66.2	86.5	91.3	74.7	92.5
House owning ratio (%)	80.6	76.6	79.1	77.3	81.2	88.7	73.2

	Workers' households (average)	of which (Quintile group of amount of savings)					
		I ~215[c]	II 215~541	III 541~1005	IV 1005~1913	V 1913~	
Engel's coefficient[e] (%)	21.7	23.6	22.7	21.9	20.6	19.2	(21.7)
Propensity to consume[f]	73.1	71.7	70.8	71.8	72.0	75.9	(73.1)

[a] All households are those with two or more persons including agricultural households; Engel's coefficient and propensity to consume are values on workers' households (with two or more persons). See Table 11.2, notes for [b–f]

Source: SB of MIAC (c) (2007), Tables 3 and 6.

11.3 Pension

Many Japanese people have lost faith in the Japanese pension system. A great percent of people do not pay the insurance fee for the national pension, which was about 36.1 percent in fiscal year 2007.[2] They have a pessimistic view regarding the future of payments. The birth rate (the total fertility rate[3]) had largely decreased to 1.26 (the lowest, 2005), and then we saw some reverse (1.37 in 2008). An aging society is approaching Japan at an extremely rapid rate and the percentage of 65-year-olds and older people exceeded 22.1 percent in (2008), which was the highest in the world. Japan will experience difficulty paying out insurance annuity funds in the future.

The government took these circumstances seriously, and planned to raise the insurance collection rate. The office of the Social Insurance Agency improperly granted a huge number of exemptions from insurance contribution. Improper insurance collection amounted to 350,000 cases in 2006. In addition to these, the loss of 50 million retirement benefit records was reported. This created great distrust of the Japanese pension system among the public. The government immediately called for an investigation and reforms to the system. Despite the strenuous effort of the government, some 20 million retirement benefit records remained unaccounted for as of March 2008. In the meantime, it turned out that the misappropriation of pension funds amounted to some 6.8 trillion yen during the period from fiscal 1952 to fiscal 2007. Reportedly, they were used for investment in the Pension Welfare Service Public Corporation, improvement of welfare facilities, and so on. Furthermore, some 69,000 pension records were suspected of being falsified. The investigation committee reported "workers at local offices of the Social Insurance Agency systematically falsified pension records of company employees" (November 2008). The reputation of Japanese pension system has been lost.

11.3.1 History

The Japanese state pension that covered the self-employed was established in 1961, with the universal pension system. Before then, employees of companies and public services each had their own pensions. The state pension (the basic pension) requires more than 25 years' payment of insurance fees. The full paid (40 years or more) pensioners currently receive about 66,000 yen per month (2008). The self-employed need additional insurance to cover their living expenses after retirement.

Table 11.4 shows the Japanese pension. In the initial stage, "benefits ratio to annual (male) income" was 25.1 percent. Reflecting economic growth, this percentage increased to 61.8 in 1973, then 63.6 in 2003. The table includes the government plan established in 2004. The plan was to increase the pension insurance rate to 18.30 (2017) from 13.58 (2003). Despite the increased insurance rate, the benefit ratio for a joint-life annuity will decrease to 50.2 percent (2023) from 59.3 percent (2004). The benefit ratio for a joint-life annuity means "a monthly pension payment/

Table 11.4 Japanese pension (employees)

Year	Model pension benefits (¥)[a]	Insurance rate (%)[b]	Average income (male) by remuneration Class(¥)	Benefits ratio to annual income (%)
1961	3,519	3.5	(1960)14,000	25.1
1973	52,242	7.6	84,600	61.8
2003 (under plan)	233,300	13.58 annually up (0.354)	367,000	63.6(59.3)[c]
2017		fixed at 18.30		
2023				(50.2)

[a]A (married) couple. [b]Split half between labor and management. [c]Percent in parentheses is the benefit ratio for a joint-life annuity, which means "a monthly pension payment/monthly after-tax income of the current standard family"

Sources: *Nihon Keizai Shinbun* (Japanese Economic Newspaper) dated November 28, 2003 based on the sources of MHLW and the Pension Fund Association; February 10, 2004 based on the second provisional calculation of MHLW

monthly after-tax income of the standard family." This plan gave people a negative idea of how the pension system might work in the future. The birth rate declined to 1.26 in 2005, which was lower than that based on the system reform. A revision of the system is expected in the near future unless the birth rate revives. It is argued that the plan was based on a more optimistic assumption of the birth rate (1.39).

11.3.2 Serious Concerns

During this period, serious improprieties were widely reported. First, pension funds were about 150 trillion yen (2003). A large amount was loaned to government-funded corporations, of which 24 out of 27 experienced difficulty in paying back interest without additional loans at the end of March 2000. About 40 percent of the pension reserve had a high possibility of becoming bad-performing loans. Final responsibility rested on the government. (Nihon Keizai Shinbun (Japanese Economic Newspaper) dated October 19, 2003 "Nenkin o Tou (4).") The unpaid rate of national pension insurance amounted to some 37.2 percent in fiscal year 2002 (worst peak until fiscal year 2007).

Second, corporations were worrying about the burden of the increased insurance rate, as the payments were evenly split between labor and management. Table 11.5 shows the survey result by the Japan Federation of Economic Organizations (*JFEO*) (2003). The result that reflected the stagnated period of economy was so pessimistic that the insurance rate deprived large corporations almost half of their profits and brought negative profits for small- and medium-size business firms (see Table 11.5). On the other hand, there was still optimism that there could be productivity growth.

Third, according to the survey of MHLW, the aged population (65 years and over) without pension amounted to 450,000 in 2005, of which about 60 percent depended

Table 11.5 Survey by the Japan federation of economic organizations (2003)

Assumption Insurance rate	Profits	Corporation size
15%	negative	Small and medium
18%	half	Big corporation (above billion capital)

Note: Survey based on the preceding 5-year financial reports
Source: *Nihon Keizai Shinbun* (Japanese Economic Newspaper) dated
October 20, 2003 "Nenkin o Tou (5)"

on the livelihood protection. The number of aged recipients of livelihood protection without pension doubled during the years 1998–2005. (*Nihon Keizai Shinbun*, dated January 22, 2008).

11.3.3 A Possible Solution

In any event, reform of the pension system is necessary. Some thoughts of possible solutions for pension reform are as follows: First is the promotion of discussion regarding the actual and legal retirement age at 65 years. In 2006, the government decided to extend the retirement age, in stages to 65 years (until 2013), by giving three options to corporations: (1) reemployment after retirement, (2) continuous employment up to age 65, and (3) the abolishment of the provisions of the retirement age. A fairly large number of companies have introduced the first case among these options (as of 2009).

Considering the pension fund, the government should further postpone pension payments as well as extend the retirement age. For this purpose, an introduction of flexible working options is helpful, such as working on a part-time or full-time basis. The average Japanese life expectancy is 83 years: 86 years for female and 79 years for male (2007). Some EU member countries have been examining the postponement of the pension payment age. For example, the German government decided (in 2009) to extend the starting age for pension payments in stages to age 67 until 2029.

Second, since pension payment is unavoidable, forming a stable pension system is the responsibility of the government. Sociologist Donald Dore mentions that, in the past, aged Japanese expected to be cared for by their children and the pension system is just the socialization of their expectations. He presents his solution: "The government collects a tax as special consumption tax for the aged to cover 90 percent of pension funds. We may consider this tax as the rent payment for social overhead capital invested by the parents' generation." (*Nihon Keizai Shinbun* dated December 29, 2003, "Interview.") The government's share of contributions to the national pension funds was one-third, but in 2004 the government decided to increase its share to one-half until 2009. According to the government estimate for the fiscal year 2003, 6.6 percent of the consumption tax was needed to cover the entire funds.

This chapter dealt with important economic issues of households and Japanese pension. By using *Household Savings Survey* and its continued revised survey, we observed structural changes to the Japanese household (1960–2005). Some of the observations were decreasing trend of family size, aging of household head, increases of yearly income and family savings, safety-oriented savings portfolio, majority of below-average savings households (two-thirds), and so on.

Then we observed the current household structure in Japan by income quintile group. Some interesting properties were that the top quintile group had the largest family size and the largest averaged number of earners. The highest average age of household head was the first (lowest) income quintile group, followed by the second income group.

Another issue was pension. Despite the grand revision of the pension system in 2004, a large number of people mistrusted the Japanese pension system. The unpaid insurance fee for the national pension was very high at 36.1 percent in 2007. The real unpaid rate, which included the number of exemptions and postponement of insurance collection, was far greater at 52.7 percent. Some improprieties were exposed. As a result, the opposition parties experienced a landslide victory in the Upper House election in 2007. There have been heated debates regarding the pension issue and another grand revision is in order.

We need to consider the pension situation as part of the social security question. The government budget on social security-related issues has been growing each year and accounts for 26.2 percent of the general government account in 2008. Social insurances (health-care insurance, nursing care expenses insurance, and pension) account for 80.4 percent of the social security-related budget, followed by livelihood protection at 9.2 percent, and social welfare at 7.6 percent. Medicare budget (medical expenses from the National Treasury), among others, occupies about 40 percent of the total budget (social security expenses), which is larger than that of pension and nursing care expenses insurance, respectively. (see Ikeda 2008, Chapter 3) About 60 percent of aged nonpensioners (65 year and over) were recipients of livelihood protection in 2007. This undermines the official stance of the Japanese universal pension system. Individual problems in the social security system should be individually solved, but the budget problems need to be considered as a part of the social security system.

The National Council on Social Security, an advisory panel to the prime minister, was established for this purpose in January 2008, and a final report was released in November 2008. The council discussed all these contributing factors and presented alternative estimates that essentially mean the government will need additional revenues[4] to reform the system.

Notes

1. Table 11.1 shows one-person households. One-person households have greatly increased, amounting to 28.2 percent of the total households (2007). For an interpretation of the results, the small number of tabulated single households should be noted (712, 704 in 2006 and 2007, respectively). When we consider the entire type of households, we need to take an

equivalence-based income. The equivalence income is defined as household income divided by the square root of household size (the number of persons). This is one of the standard ways of adjustment of the difference of household size. Since the 2001 survey, *FIES<Income and Expenditure>* (SB of MIAC (b)) includes one-person households. Note that *FIES <Savings and Liabilities>* (SB of MIAC (c)) is restricted to two or more member households.

2. The unpaid rate of insurance fee increased to the highest 37.2 percent in 2002, when the insurance fee collection department was transferred from the local government to the central government (social insurance office). If we include the number of exemptions and postponement of insurance collection, the real unpaid rate of insurance increases to 52.7 percent (2007). This real unpaid rate has increased for the sixth consecutive year since 2003.

3. The total fertility rate is defined as the average number of live births for all women between the ages of 15 and 49.

4. According to the estimate, the government needs, under the current pension system based on the insurance fee, about 3.3 to 3.5 percentage points in the consumption tax rate by fiscal 2015. If entire funds were covered by the consumption tax, the government would need 6–11 percentage points tax rate in fiscal 2015. (*Nihon Keizai Shinbun* (Japanese Economic Newspaper) dated November 5, 2008)

Chapter 12
Toward the Quality of Life in the Mature Society (Summary and Lessons)

The final chapter has a brief summary and then we briefly outline a proposal for a basic design towards achieving high satisfaction level society. The quality of life in the mature society is the direction in which all policies should lead. This is a society that we should aspire to in the future.

12.1 A Brief Summary

In the introduction, we explained the intention of this book, which is well expressed by the title "*Postwar Japanese Economy: Lessons of Economic Growth and the Bubble Economy.*" We gave a brief political and economic landscape. Then using our rough classification of the average growth rate, the economic landscape by period was examined. As an important lesson from our study, we proposed a welfare-oriented society that leads to our goal, "the high quality of life in the mature society."

Chapter 2 presented historical changes of the Japanese postwar economy from various points by figures and tables. We analyzed the remarkable changes in the Japanese economy, and, among others, the most remarkable phenomenon was economic growth. We observed that economic growth brought great structural changes both in the production by industry and the labor force by industry and status in employment. We also examined the labor force status (unemployment), price increases, income, income distribution, and international concern. International concern included the exchange rate, trade balance, and foreign direct investment.

In Chapter 3, we explained major reforms and other important social and political changes, and in particular economic policy immediately after World War II. These reforms were carried out under the allied occupation and were important foundations for establishing strong economic growth in Japan. Major reforms (antitrust measures—the dissolution of Zaibatsu—land reform, labor reform, and tax reform) and social and political changes contributed to the democratization of Japan economically and politically, although each of these brought some chaotic situations in the beginning. Despite the strenuous effort of the government, it was the Dodge Plan that finally tamed inflation. As a result, Japan went into a severe deflationary

M. Iyoda, *Postwar Japanese Economy*, DOI 10.1007/978-1-4419-6332-1_12,
© Springer Science+Business Media, LLC 2010

spiral, but the severe recession was averted by the special export demand created by the Korean War (June 1950).

In Chapter 4, we observed some outstanding facts and then dealt with general backgrounds and some reasons for the rapid growth and the government policy at the time. First, we explained the underpinnings of the period by dividing it into political, international, and domestic business backgrounds. Second, we discussed some reasons for the rapid economic growth including (1) wide and huge technology improvements, (2) the high savings rate, and (3) the low expense costs of the defense forces. Third was the government policy. *EPA* was charged with macroeconomic policy, proposing indicative plans that stimulated actual growth. *MITI* was charged with industrial policy, and guided it by setting target industries, which contributed to the rapid growth. For the foreign economic policy, a free trade policy was established but with capital control against foreign investment, infant industry protection, and a fixed exchange rate.

Chapter 5 dealt with positive results of economic growth. The great results were a huge *GNP* and a high per capita *GNP*. Reflecting income growth, we observed the high growth rate of durable consumer goods, increased livelihood protection, establishment and improvement of the universal pension and health insurance, the accumulation of social overhead capital, and improvement of income distribution. These were all positive effects of economic growth.

Chapter 6 dealt with the negative results of economic growth. The implementation of infrastructures was unbalanced; that is, social imbalance between the private and public investment increased during the rapid economic growth period, causing and intensifying negative results or distortions in economic growth. Concentration of population to metropolitan areas caused serious problems for both the depopulated and overpopulated areas. Environmental disruption was extremely serious. Inflation brought instability to the poor groups in the society. We also discussed the plight of people left behind by the advancing times. All of these negative costs were huge. The government belatedly attempted various countermeasures to address the growing problems, particularly the depopulated areas and pollution.

Chapters 7 and 8 dealt with the bubble economy and its consequences. Once the bubble phenomenon began, it spread rapidly. There were major causes that accumulated, particularly in the early 1980s, to generate the ever-increasing bubble. Japan had a huge trade surplus, and many corporations had obtained huge amounts of money by issuing equities or bonds with low interest rates. In this environment, the Plaza Accord caused a greater appreciation of the yen to the dollar and a serious shock to the Japanese exporting industries, resulting in depression.

As a result, the Japanese policy authorities adopted monetary and fiscal policies to cope with these hardships. These included the low interest rate and spending plans aimed at expanding domestic demand. These made a triggering role, under which "impact loans" greatly contributed to the generation of the bubble economy. Japan's accumulated money (capital) was used to partly fund the capital exports but mainly went into speculative markets such as land and shares. The Japan–US Structural Impediments Initiative talks intensified the abovementioned government policies.

We reviewed the economic cost of the bubble economy, including the deterioration of income and asset distribution, housing problems, and serious distortions in the resource allocations.

After the bubble economy, Japan's economy suffered from a period of stagnation brought on by huge bad loans in Japanese banks and outstanding government bonds. The industrial hollowing-out of Japan was accelerated. Various reasons have been given for the lost age; however, among others, the following might be important: (1) Many economists and policy authorities lacked sufficient recognition of the seriousness of "stock adjustments." (2) The Japanese economy could not effectively adjust to worldwide globalization. Long overdue changes were needed in the Japanese style of labor management and business policies. In a sense, Japan's success contributed to a series of setbacks to its economy in the 1990s and early 2000s.

Chapter 9 dealt with some lessons from rapid economic growth and the bubble economy. The Japanese thought that economic growth meant a bright future; however, the costs were higher, though they obtained more goods and services. Such expectations were based on *GNP* growth forecasts. To equate the growth of *GNP* with that of economic welfare was seriously questioned. We explained some of the weaknesses of this concept such as market failures in its measurement and distortions or limitations from the welfare viewpoint.

To measure welfare, *NNW* or *NEW* and the like were constructed by revising *GNP*. And in a further development, we now have the *GPI*, social indicators, and the measurement of happiness. We showed that the gap between the per capita *GDP* and per capita *GPI* has become wider ever since the mid-1970s. This fact is critically important. We showed our integrated idea for welfare-oriented society. We use the current GDP index as a measure of market activity, but the concrete policy should be judged from whether or not it is GPI enhancing. We also consider some of the important findings of happiness research.

Additional lessons from the Japanese bubble experience include (1) giving fair information promptly and widely, (2) preparing for the hedge environment as much as possible, (3) establishing business ethics and fostering the spirit of compliance, and (4) ensuring international cooperation to complement the market imperfection under the current information society. Costs of the bubble before and after were serious and extremely large, which made for a deteriorating effect on the welfare of the society. As Soros mentioned, global capitalism has intrinsic instability and generating the bubble was unavoidable. There are two ways to deal with such situations: one is to have policy controls and market regulations, which may relax or weaken the effect of the bubble, and the other way is to set a safety net for people facing everyday difficulties or are the victims of economic fluctuations or disasters.

Chapters 10 and 11 dealt with some important economic issues that may have a direct relationship to the welfare-oriented society. Chapter 10 dealt with income and asset distribution, and the relative share of income. Income distribution has been deteriorating in Japan and the United States and the United Kingdom since the 1980s. For Japan, however, a major reason is its aging demographics (aging society greatly affected by the baby boom generation). Japanese inequality of income distribution seems to be slightly higher than the average of the *OECD* member nations. It is not easy to show the asset distribution trend, particularly real asset distribution, but we presented the two important properties: the J-shape relationship between income and holding asset values, and the weight and meaning of bequests in Japan. For the relative share of labor, the properties are as follows: (1) It fluctuates countercyclically. (2) It is generally low during the rapid growth period and vice versa for the slow growth period. (3) The share in manufacturing industries is generally lower than in nonmanufacturing industries. (4) The share in small- and medium-size companies is far higher than in big corporations.

Chapter 11 dealt with households and pension. We observed the structural changes of the Japanese household since 1960. Various properties were observed such as the continuous decrease in family size, increased age of household head, greater increase in savings, safety-oriented savings portfolios, and decrease in Engel's coefficient. We then observed current household structure by quintile, of which we found some interesting properties. Observations by quintile are not the same as those by average aggregate.

The Japanese universal pension system began in 1961. But as a result of the rapidly aging society, the Japanese pension system faced a critical problem of balancing pension funds and future payments. Furthermore several pension scandals were reported therefore, the government has lost the trust of its people regarding the Japanese pension system. Restructuring the pension system is now a necessity, and should be considered as a total system overhaul that includes the retirement age (with a flexible option of work), the insurance rate, the government share of contribution, and payments, all as part of the social security system.

12.2 Toward a Welfare-Oriented Society

12.2.1 *Enhancing* GPI

The first step toward constructing a welfare-oriented society is to show the methodology.

What can we learn through these analyses? Economic growth is important in general, and particularly at a certain per capita income level. After that, economic growth may not be essential, and the living satisfaction level becomes more important. As far as economic growth is expressed by the current *GDP*, we should recognize the distortions or limitations of this concept. The government has measured *GDP* every year, having used it for government policy decisions. We should give top priority to enhancing the *GPI*, from which viewpoint we select a policy. *GPI* is formed from the welfare viewpoint by revising *GDP*. Happiness is a more comprehensive concept, of which it is not easy to make an integrated definite policy system, so we place more importance on the *GPI* concept. However, important findings of happiness research should be taken into consideration such as threshold income for the living satisfaction and importance of good institutions. Government policies to protect against market failures and for social balance may increase the *GPI*, narrowing the gap between the *GPI* and *GDP*.

As we mentioned in Chapter 9, Hamilton (2003) proposed "eudemonism" as an alternative political program. Our welfare-oriented society is not at such a point in its evolution. But happiness would be the final and eternal purpose of human life. In this respect, we can share "eudemonism" with Hamilton. A welfare-oriented society would be a more concrete, restricted, but plausible concept.

The Stiglitz-led commission report (Stiglitz, Sen and Fitoussi (eds.) 2009)[1] is inclined to favor this methodological presentation. Stiglitz says that national income statistics such as *GDP* and *GNP* were "originally intended as a measure of market economic activity, including the public sector," which is not a measure of societal wellbeing. The current national accounts are flawed statistics, so Stiglitz proposes reforms that will better measure wellbeing. "What we measure affects what we do. If we have the wrong metrics, we will strive for the wrong things. In the quest to increase *GDP*, we may end up with a society in which most citizens have become worse off." He also says, "*GDP* will, of course, continue to be used as a measure of market activity, though hopefully the reforms that we propose will make it a better measure of that." The idea is not the first of its type, but it struck a global chord with the most comprehensive assessment of limitations of existing data. What is sensible is Mr. Sarkozy's initiative as president of France. "Happiness, long holidays and a sense of wellbeing may not be everyone's yardstick for economic performance, but Nicolas Sarkozy believes that they should be embraced by the world in a national accounting overhaul" (Ben Hall). He urged other countries to adopt proposed new measures of economic output.

12.2.2 Some Important Factors Dealt with in Chapters 10 and 11

The second step to construct a welfare-oriented society is to study important factors and actual conditions that may relate to this society. We dealt with income and asset distribution, relative share of labor, household structure, and pension as important factors.

A policy study should be carried out based on the current condition of households. For the time being, demographics is a key factor in which to consider income and asset distribution, and pension. These matters should be considered in connection with households. The study of household structure will be needed.

There are two types of policies affecting personal distribution. The first type is a so-called income redistribution policy that is carried out through the taxation system and social security. After-tax income distribution is not so bad in Japan (see Fig. 2.4). Asset distribution should be dealt with in connection with bequests. The second is a policy of equalizing income sources, which is carried out through equal asset holding, equal educational opportunities, and equal opportunity in employment. This kind of policy will be increasingly necessary for the establishment of a society with high-level satisfaction. We have not had a systematic policy influencing functional distribution, although it is generally considered that some policies bring full employment and keep price stable and that some industrial policies relate to this.

Despite the grand revision of the pension system in 2004, the Japanese pension system has lost public trust. And in fact, there is demand for yet another revision of the pension system. We need to consider the pension situation as part of the social security issue. Individual problems in the social security system should be individually solved, but the budget problems should be considered in the overall social security system.

12.3 Quality of Life in the Mature Society

12.3.1 Systemic Design

Towards establishing a satisfied society, we need a systemic design, that is the quality of life[2] in the **mature society**. The mature society is a society that has attained a high level of income and can afford a healthy, satisfied, and culturally enriched way of living. Most *OECD* member countries fall into this category as their per capita *GNI* in terms of *ppp*1995 exceeds US\$10,000.

The quality of life in the mature society is that of a welfare-oriented society, which has three important properties. First is the safety net.[3] The society prepares for the social security of its individuals with livelihood protection, medical insurance, and pension. When an individual person or a family has difficulty sustaining their way of living, (including unemployment, sickness, the physically impaired, and the death of household head, the aged, fires, and natural disasters) they are relieved under that safety net. The net also includes countermeasures to prevent market failure and to promote the market economy (government policy). A safety net for financial market is an example, as it prevents market destruction and promotes an efficient working market. For this we have a deposit insurance system and the central bank as the "last resort of lending."

The government serves a major function in this safety net, but corporations and households also play a role. The latter examples for the corporation are social insurance contributions which include health, employment, pension, and workmen's accident compensation, and an effective working environment for the elderly. The role of the household is to help keep the elderly in their own homes to look after them as much as possible. The safety net can result in "a moral hazard," which means the system can be abused. Examples include easy dole dependence, tax evasion, and excessive medical treatment under the health insurance.

Another important property is a safe society, which has low crime rates, is pollution free, has fewer traffic accident, safe foods, and so on. For these purposes, the improvement of public services is needed. The final property is keeping social balance between privately produced goods and services and those of the public sector. We should consider the huge costs incurred by the social maladies and economic problems caused by social imbalance.

12.3.2 Some Important Concerns

We must also discuss three important factors that affect quality of life: education, market failures, and the government. An important challenge facing us is how to synchronize our present life in the information society with our ideal society. We are surrounded by all the trappings of modern conveniences, which are often quite seductive. Our youth is especially vulnerable to such trappings, and adults are not immune either. The most important foundation on which to build our ideal society may be education in a broad sense that includes social, family, and school education. The standard of living level highly depends on individual aspirations, and this desire is insatiable without a moderate sense of life (a life balance between the material and the other),[4] which relates to the philosophy of life or the way of life.

In connection with this, various education studies are needed, among others, the study of the relationship between income distribution and education is important, particularly in the current Japanese society. A well-known fact is that intelligence quotient (*IQ*) is normal distribution, but income distribution is skewed (positive) to the right. This means median income is below the average, for very high-income people increase the average income. This fact itself should not be taken in the absolute sense because our abilities are not confined to the *IQ* test result, but are related to various factors such as physical ability, disposition, personality, leadership, and experiences. The question is what factor is the vital one in income distribution. If the decisive factor is not related to the individual character but is affected by parents' income and social status, this theory may need correction from the viewpoint of fairness. In this respect, we agree with Rawls (1971).

An Expert Panel of the Ministry of Education, Culture, Sports, Science and Technology released a survey result on the relationship of national achievement test scores and annual household income of students.[5] The release was the first of its kind. An interesting result was that all test scores in Japanese and Mathematics had a direct proportion to the parents' income until 15 million yen income group; scores of students in the above 15 million yen group were a little less than those in the 12–15 million yen group. It also turned out that scores were higher in proportion to the additional household payment for those attending tutoring schools or taking correspondence courses. Furthermore, an interesting point is that those high-scoring students and their families tended to discuss current issues/events on a regular basis.

We are now fully aware of various kinds of market failure, which is a market's inability to achieve either an optimum resource allocation or maximum economic welfare. The main sources of market failure are externalities (pollution), imperfect competition (monopoly), and public goods (supplied by the government), asymmetric information, missing markets (the absence of a market).[6] Market failures may necessitate government intervention to regulate markets through competition, regional and industrial policies, price support systems, and income distribution by correctives (minimum wage rate, agricultural policy, and progressive taxation). We can take countermeasures toward each failure. However, the market power in capitalism is strong enough and brings structural changes in the economy, causing frictions in the society. Countermeasures for any drawback in the market economy is apt to greatly lag when people put a top priority on economic growth.

For the high quality of life society, the government's role and its cost will increase. Government must ensure the efficiency of public services while cutting its cost as much as possible. However, a small government may have difficulty doing this. A high satisfaction society demands good social products (public goods) and improvement of infrastructures, and people should understand the necessary costs. In fact, instead of demanding so much service from the government, they should do more themselves individually or as a group in the community. A strong government should be constructed on people's self-reliance and non-moral hazard conscience. These attitudes and social conscience are formed through education in a broad sense and through social cohesion.

Under a welfare-oriented society, people seek happiness through shorter working hours, and may shift down from a life of excessive consumption to a less consuming prudent one with satisfaction. However, this individual effort is not always easy, for our desires are formed by various factors: cultural tradition, life style, religion, institutional property, and so on. The key to have a satisfied life is how to control one's aspirations.

12.3.3 International Concern

In addition to the above-mentioned, factors, we need to consider economic stability domestically and internationally as an important target. This is an important lesson that we have learned as a result of the bubble economy.

Domestically each country has its responsibility to stabilize the economy, avoiding extreme results. However, countries are interlocked in the world economy through international trade and capital transactions. Global capitalism has intrinsic instability, so maintaining economic stability is sometimes a hard task; therefore, international cooperation is important. Summit talks are important. At the Pittsburgh summit meeting in September 2009, discussions about global economic issues shifted from the Group 7 big industrial nations to the Group of 20, which includes China, India, Brazil, South Korea, and South Africa. The big question is whether the Group of 20 will be more effective, or whether it will simply be more unwieldy. However, without international cooperation, an internationally interwoven world economy would not be stabilized.

There are various international organizations such as the *IMF*, *WTO*, World Bank and *OECD*, which have played an important role in the development and stability of the world economy. Further roles are expected, particularly from the *IMF*. Local monetary cooperation would be also useful such as Chieng-Mai initiative. The Chieng-Mai initiative is an agreement by the Ministers of Finance of *ASEAN* (Association of Southeast Asian Nations), Japan, China, and Korea in May 2005 that calls for the steady cooperation through swap agreements[7] between two countries. As a result of the bitter experiences of the Asian monetary crisis, these countries realized that the degree of damage could be weakened if they had had more cooperative relationships among the Asian countries. (see Jiyu Kokumin-sha 2009, pp. 466–7)

Soros (1998) mentioned, "One deficiency was the lack of adequate international supervisory and regulatory authority" (p. 179). "There are no permanent and comprehensive solutions" toward avoiding a financial crisis. He continues, "One thing is certain: Financial markets are inherently unstable; they need supervision and regulation" (Soros 1998, p. 194). We need much ingenuity to complement the market imperfection under the current information technology. We do not know the best solution for this now, but we should do our best toward solving this dilemma. Society as well as the country learns more through painful experiences rather than through easygoing prosperous experiences. We should consider the huge cost that we have had to pay as a tuition fee in life's lessons.

Notes

1. The Commission on the Measurement of Economic Performance and Social Progress (*CMEPSP*)) chaired by Joseph Stiglitz, a Nobel prize-winning professor at Columbia University, released a final report in September 2009. The Commission was set up in 2008 at the request of Nicolas Sarkozy, president of France, who was concerned about popular distrust of economic statistics. Professor Stiglitz chaired and another Nobel prizewinner, Amartya Sen, at Harvard University served as adviser, and Professor Jean-Paul Fitoussi of the Institut d'Etudes Politiques de Paris served as coordinator. (see *Financial Times*, "Towards a better measure of well-being (by Joseph Stiglitz)," September 14, 2009 and "Sarkozy strives for measure of happiness (by Ben Hall)," September 15, 2009).
2. Stiglitz et al. (eds.) (2009, pp. 14–15) define wellbeing and refer to the quality of life from the comprehensive viewpoint. Wellbeing at least in principle should simultaneously consider the following eight dimensions: material living standard; health; education; personal activities including work; political voice and governance; social connections and relationships; environment; insecurity. Quality of life depends on people's objective conditions and capabilities. Quality of life indicators in all the dimensions covered should assess inequality in a comprehensive way.
3. The safety net is a net that not only relieves economically disadvantaged people but also prevents market failure and smoothly promotes the market economy. The expression is derived from a safety net laid under circus tightrope walkers.
4. A moderate sense is not a definite expression, which means not go to the extreme but to keep balance. We consider that, under the current affuluent society, the balance should be more on the non-material side. A sense of life is fundamentally guided by the individual philosophy or way of life that is broadly formed through education.
5. The panel surveyed 6th grade elementary students (8,093) in 100 public schools of ordinance-designated cities (major cities nationwide) in Japan and their parents' income (household income, 5,847 replied) in school year 2008. For 12–15 million yen income households, the scores in basic knowledge of Japanese and Mathematics was 8 points above the average, respectively; for the less than 2 million yen income households, the scores were 10 points below the average. The score differences between the low- and the high-income groups in both subjects were far greater in application questions of basic knowledge. (see *Nihon Keizai Shinbun* (Japanese Economic Newspaper) on August 5, 2009, "The Difference of the Test Score Caused by the Household Income" (in Japanese).)
6. Externality is defined as a cost or benefit arising from any activity that does not accrue to the person or organization carrying out the activity (pollution, fertilization of fruit trees by bees).

Asymmetric information is a situation where information is unevenly distributed between the parties to a contract or transaction.

7. Swap agreement is a reciprocal currency agreement to deposit reciprocally the countries' currency between the central banks. When it is needed to intervene in the foreign currency market, the foreign currency is obtained within the pre-agreed amount.

References

CAO of GoJ (Cabinet Office, Government of Japan) (2002–2007, English ed.). *Annual Report on the Japanese Economy and Public Finance*. Tokyo: National Printing Bureau. (Note that there is one year lag of publication between the Japanese and English Editions except for 2004 and 2005 editions. See also EPA of GoJ (b) (–2001)).

Clark, C.G (1940). *The Conditions of Economic Growth*. London: Macmillan.

Crystal, D. (ed.) (2004). *The Pengin Encyclopedia*, 2nd ed. London: Pengin Books Ltd.

Economist (2008). *Japain*, why Japan keeps failing, *The Economists*, February 23rd, pp. 27–30.

Environment Agency (1976). *Quality of the Environment in Japan, 1976*. Tokyo: Printing Bureau, Ministry of Finance.

Environmental Dispute Coordination Committee (1999, 2007, 2009). *Kogai Funso Shori Hakusho* [White Paper on the Settlement of Environmental Pollution Dispute]. Tokyo: National Printing Bureau.

EPA (Economic Planning Agency), GoJ (Government of Japan) (b) (–2001, English ed.). *Economic Survey of Japan*. Tokyo: Printing Bureau, Ministry of Finance. (Note that there is a year lag of publication between the Japanese and English editions).

EPA (Economic Planning Agency), GoJ (Government of Japan) (c) (1994). *Kokumin Seikatsu Hakusho* [White Paper on National Living Life]. Tokyo: Printing Bureau, Ministry of Finance.

Förster, M. and Mira d'Ercole, M. (2005). Income Distribution and Poverty in OECD Countries in the Second Half of the 1990s, OECD Social, Employment and Migration Working Papers, 22, pp. 1–79.

FSA (Financial Services Agency), Japanese Government (1998). Yokin Toriatsukai Kikan no Risuku Kanri no Jokyo-toh nitsuite [The State of Loans under the Risk Management in Deposit Taking Financial Institutions] (www.fsa.go.jp/p_fsa/news/newsj2/news-j-717.html).

Frey, B.S and Stutzer, A. (2002a). What Can Economist Learn from Happiness Research? *Journal of Economic Literature*, 60(June), 402–435.

Frey, B.S. and Stutzer, A. (2002b). *Happiness and Economics: How the Economy and Institutions Effect Human Wellbeing*. Princeton: Princeton University Press. Japanese version translated by Fuyuhi Sawasaki supervised by Takamitsu Sawa (2005). *Kofuku no Seiji-Keizaigaku: Hitobito no Shiawase o Sokushin surumono wa Nanika*. Tokyo: Daiyamondo-sha.

Fukuda, J. (ed.) (2009). *Nihon no Zaisei, 2009 ed.* [Japanese Finance]. Tokyo: Toyo Keizai Shinpo-sha.

Gakkai, S. (1995). *Sengo Nihon Sangyoshi* [Postwar Japanese History of Industry]. Tokyo: Toyo Keizai Shinpo-sha.

Galbraith, J.K. (1998). *The Affluent Society*. New York: Houghton Mifflin Company. Japanese version translated by Tetsutaro Suzuki (2006). *Yutaka na Shakai* (kettei-ban). Tokyo: Iwanami Shoten.

Hamilton, C. (2003). *Growth Fetish*. Crows Nest, Australia: Allen & Unwin Australia Pty Ltd. Japanese version translated by Yoichi Shimada (2004). *Keizai Seicho no Shinwa karano Dakkyaku*. Tokyo: Aspect.

Hamilton, C and Dennis R. (2000). Tracking Well-being in Australia: The Genuine Progress Indicator 2000, Discussion Paper, No. 34. Canberra: Australian Association.

Harada, Y. and Kosai, Y. (1987). *Nihon Keizai Hatten no Big Game: Rent Seeking Katsudo o Koete* [A Big Game of the Japanese Economic Development: Beyond the Rent Seeking Activity]. Tokyo: Toyo Keizai Shinpo-sha.

Hayashi, N. (ed.) (2007). *Nihon no Zaisei, 2007 ed.* [Japanese Finance]. Tokyo: Toyo Keizai Shinpo-sha.

HCLC (Holding Company Liquidation Commission) (1973). *Nihon Zaibatsu to Sono Kaitai* (1) [Japanese Zaibatsu and the Dissolution (1)] (Meiji Hyakunenshi Sohsho, Vol. 221). Tokyo: Hara Shobo.

Helliwell, J.F. (2001). How's Life? Combining Individual and National Variables to Explain Subjective Well-Being, mimeo, U British Columbia. Printed in (2003) *Economic Modeling*, 20(2), 331–360.

Helliwell, J.F. and Huang, H. (2006). How's Your Government? International Evidence Linking Good Government and Well-Being. NBER Working Papers, No. 11988, January.

Horioka, C.Y., Yamahira, K., Nishikawa, M., and Iwamoto, S. (2002). Nihonjin no Isan Doki no Jyuyodo, Seishitsu, Eikyo nitsuite, [On the Importance, Properties and Influence of the Japanese Bequest Motive], *Yusei Kenkyu-sho Geppo*, 163, 4–31.

Hsu, R.C. (1999). *The MIT Encyclopedia of the Japanese Economy*, 2nd ed. Cambrigde, MA: The MIT Press.

Ichinose, A. (1999). The Bubble and Monetary Policy in Japan: 1984–1989, *Okayama Economic Review*, 31(3), 1–33.

Ichinose, A. (2005). *Josho: Nihon no Bubble Saikou* [Introductory Chapter: The Japanese Bubble Economy Reconsidered]. In Atsushi Ichinose (ed.), *Gendai Kinyu Kiki no Kaimei* [An Analysis of the Modern Financial Crisis]. Kyoto: Mineruva Shobo.

Ikeda, A. (ed.) (2008). *Nihon no Zaisei, 2008 ed.* [Japanese Finance]. Tokyo: Toyo Keizai Shinpo-sha.

Investigation Committee of the General Policy Division, National Life Council (1985). *Kokumin Seikatsu Shihyo [NSI* (New Social Indicators)]. Tokyo: National Printing Bureau.

Ishizaki, T. (1983). *Nihon no Shotoku to Tomi no Bunpai* [Income and Asset Distribution of Japan]. Tokyo: Toyo Keizai Shinpo-sha.

Ito, T (1992). *The Japanese Economy*. Cambridge, MA: The MIT Press.

Itoh, M. (2000). *Japanese Economy Reconsidered.* New York: Palgrave.

Iyoda, M. (1984). Kojin Kigyo Bumon no Nichi-Ei Hikaku (1950–1982) [A Comparative Study of the Self-employed Businesses between Japan and the United Kingdom, 1950–1982], *Economic and Business Review* (St. Andrew's University, Osaka), 26(1), 55–83.

Iyoda, M. (1987). Sengo Nihon no Rodo Bunpai-ritsu 1950–1985 [Estimation of Relative Income Shares of Labour in Postwar Japan 1950–1985], *Bulletin of Research Institute* (St. Andrew's University, Osaka), 13(2), 1–10.

Iyoda, M. (1991). Sengo Nihon no Jinteki Shotoku Bunpai: Kinro-sha Setai o Chushin ni Survey [Personal Distribution of Income in Postwar Japan: Survey on Workers' Households], *Bulletin of the Research Institute* (St. Andrew's University, Osaka), 16(3), 25–36.

Iyoda, M. (1997). *Profits, Wages, and Productivity in the Business Cycle: A Kaldorian Analysis.* Boston, MA: Kluwer.

Iyoda, M. (2006). *Makuro Keizaigaku* [Macroeconomics], 2nd ed. Kyoto: Horitsu Bunka-sha.

Iyoda, M. (2008). Towards a High Quality of Life Society: GDP, Welfare and Happiness, *Economic and Business Review* (St. Andrew's University, Osaka), 49(4), 123–138.

Jackson, T., Marks, N., Ralls, J., and Stymne, S. (1997). *An Index Of Sustainable Economic Welfare for the UK: 1950–1996.* Guildford: Environment Strategy Centre, Surrey University.

Kokumin-sha, J. (ed.) (1976). *Gendai Yougo no Kiso Chishiki* [Basic Knowledge of Modern Terminology]. Tokyo: Jiyu Kokumin-sha.

Kanamori, H., Ara, K., and Moriguchi, C. (eds.) (2002). *Yuhikaku Dictionary of Economic Terms,* 4th ed. Tokyo: Yuhikaku.

Kanamori, H., Ara, K., and Moriguchi, C., Shinohara, Miyohei., Tachi, Ryutaro., Tsujimura, Kotaro. and Miyazawa, Kimio (eds.) (1981). *Nihon Keizai Jiten* [Dictionary of the Japanese Economy]. Tokyo: Nihon Keizai Shinbun-sha.

Keynes, J.M. (1936). *The General Theory of Employment, Interest and Money*. London: Macmillan.

Komiya, R. (1975). *Gendai Nihon Keizai Kenkyu* [Studies of Modern Japanese Economy]. Tokyo: University of Tokyo Press.

Kosai, Y. (2007). Symposium: Nihon Keizai—Kako, Ima and Mirai [Symposium: The Japanese Economy—Past, Now and Future]. Nihon Keizai Shinbun, November 19, 2007.

Koshiro, K. (2000). *A Fifty Year History of Industry and Labor in Postwar Japan*. Tokyo: Japan Institute of Labor.

Kuznets, S. (1955). Economic Growth and Income Inequality, *American Economic Review*, 45(1), 1–28.

Kuznets, S. (1963). Quantitative Aspects of Economic Growth of Nations: VIII Distribution Income by Size, *Economic Development and Cultural Change*, (January) 11(s2), 1–37.

Mogbel, Zahal (2005). "Nihon Keizai no Globaruka wa Kano ka: Tainichi Chokusetsu Toshi to Globaruka o Megutte," [The Possibility of Globalization of the Japanese Economy: Foreign Direct Investment and Globalization]. In Atsushi Ichinose (ed.), *Gendai Kinyu-Keizai Kiki no Kaimei* [A Clarification of the Modern Monetary and Economic Crisis] (pp. 269–297). Kyoto: Mineruva Shobo.

Morita, M. (1961). Shihon Chikuseki to Kokka no Shisaku [Capital Accumulation and National Policy]. In Shigeru, A. (ed.), *Gendai Nihon no Shihon Chikuseki* [Capital Accumulation in Modern Japan]. Tokyo: University of Tokyo Press.

Nakamura, T. (1995). *The Postwar Japanese Economy: Its Development and Structure*, 2nd ed. Tokyo: University of Tokyo Press. Japanese original edition (1993), *Nihon Keizai: Sono Seicho to Kozo*, 2nd ed. Tokyo: University of Tokyo Press.

Nakano, K. and Yoshikawa, E. (2006). Genuine Progress Indicator: Features and Futures, *Hikone Ronso*, 357, 175–193.

Nakatani, I. (2007). *Nyumon Macro Keizaigaku*, 5th ed. [Introduction to Macroeconomics]. Tokyo: Nihon Hyoron-sha.

Nishizaki, K. and Sugou, T. (2001). Wagakuni ni okeru Rodo Bunpairitsu ni tsuite no Ichi- Kousatsu [A Study of the Relative Share of Labour of Japan], BoJ Working Paper (01–08), pp. 1–51.

NNW Development Committee, Economic Council (1973). *Atarashii Fukushi Shihyo: NNW* [New Welfare Index]. Tokyo: Printing Bureau, Ministry of Finance.

Nomura, M. (2007). *Nihon-teki Koyo Kanko* [Japanese Style of Labour-Mnagement Relationship]. Kyoto: Mineruba Shobo.

Nordhaus, W. and Tobin, J. (1971). Is Growth Obsolete? Cowles Foundation Discussion Papers 319, Cowles Foundation, Yale University. Published in (1972) *Economic Growth*, Fifties Anniversary Colloquium (NBER Series No. 96E) (pp. 1–80). New York: Columbia University Press.

OECD (–2007). *Economic Surveys: Japan*. Paris: OECD.

Ohtake, F. (1994). 1980 Nendai no Shotoku-Shisan Bunpai [Income and Asset Distribution in the 1980s], *Quarterly Journal of Econometrics and Economics*, 45(5), 385–402.

Ohtake, F. (2005). *Nihon no Fubyodo* [Japanese Inequality]. Tokyo: Nihon Keizai Shinbun-sha.

Petty, W. (1690). Political Arithmetick. In Hull, C.H. (ed.) (1889), *The Economic Writings of Sir William Petty*, Vol. 1. Cambrigde: Cambridge University Press. Reprinted ed. (1963), New York: Kelly.

Planning Bureau, EPA (Economic Planning Agency) (1975). *Shotoku Shisan Bunpai no Jittai to Mondaiten* [Realities and Questions of the Distribution of Property and Income]. Tokyo: Printing Bureau, Ministry of Finance.

QLPB (Quality-of-Life Policy Bureau) of EPA (1989). *Kokumin Seikatsu Shihyo* [National Life Indicator: *NSI* (New Social Indicators) estimate of 1989]. Tokyo: Printing Bureau, Ministry of Finance.

QLPB (Quality-of-Life Policy Bureau) of EPA (1999). *Shin Kokumin Seikatsu Shihyo, Heisei 11 nenban* [Peoples Life Indicators]. Tokyo: Printing Bureau, Ministry of Finance.

Ravallion, M. and Chen, S. (2004). Understanding China's (uneven) Progress Agaist Poverty, *Finance and Development*, 41(4), pp. 16–19.

Rawls, J. (1971; revized 1999). *A Theory of Justice*. Cambridge, MA: The Belknap Press of Harvard University Press. Japanese version translated by Kinji Yajima, supervisor (1979), *Seigiron*. Tokyo: Kinokuniya Shoten.

Robinson, J. (1960). The Theory of Distribution. In Robinson, J. *Collected Economic Papers* (Vol. 2) (pp. 145–158). Oxford: Basil Blackwell.

Sakakibara, E. (2003). *Structural Reform in Japan: Breaking the Iron Triangle*. Washington DC: Brookings Institution Press.

Samuelson, P. and Nordhaus, W.D (1989). *Economics*, 13th ed. New York: MaGraw-Hill Book Company.

Soros, G. (1998). *The Crisis of Global Capitalism: Open Society Endangered*. New York: Public Affairs. Japanese version translated by Susumu Ohara (1999), *Gurobaru Shihon-shugi no Kiki*. Tokyo: Nihon Keizai Shinbun-sha.

Stiglitz, J., Sen, A., and Fitoussi, J.-P. (eds.) (2009). *Report by the Commission on the Measurement of Economic Performance and Social Progress*. Downloaded from http://www.stiglitz-sen-fitoussi.fr/en/index.htm

Tachibanaki, T. (1998). *Nihon no Keizai Kakusa* [Economic Differencials of Japan]. Tokyo: Iwanami Shoten.

Tachibanaki, T. and Takata, S. (1994). Bequests and Asset Distribution: Human Capital Investment and Intergenerational Wealth Transfers. In Tachibanaki, T. (ed.), *Savings and Bequests*. Ann Arbor, MI: University of Michigan Press.

Tachibanaki, T. and Urakawa, K. (2006). *Nihon no Hinkon Kenkyu* [A Study of the Japanese Poverty]. Tokyo: University of Tokyo Press.

Takayama, N. (1980). *Fubyodo no Keizai Bunseki* [Economic Analysis of Inequality]. Tokyo: Toyo Keizai Shinpo-sha.

Takayama, N. and Arita, F. (1996). *Chochiku to Shisan Keisei: Kakei Shisan no Micro-data Analysis* [Savings and Asset Formation: Micro-data Analysis of Household Assets]. Hitsotsubashi University Economic Research Series No. 46. Tokyo: Iwanami Shoten.

Takenaka, H. (2008). *Structural Reforms of the Koizumi Cabinet: An Insider's Account of the Economic Revival of Japan*. Translated by Jillian Yorke from Japanese Edition (2006), *Kozo Kaikaku no Shinjitsu:Takenaka Heizo Daijin Nisshi*. Tokyo: Nihon Keizai Shinbun-sha.

Talberth, J., Cobb, C., and Slattery, N. (2007). *The Genuine Progress Indicator 2006: A Tool for Sustainable Development*. Oakland, CA: Redefining Progress. (http://www.rprogress.org/publications/2007/GPI%202006.pdf).

Tanaka, K. (1972). *Nihon Retto Kaizoron* [A Plan for Remodeling the Japanese Archipelago]. Tokyo: Nikkan Kogyo Shinbun-sha.

Tsuru, S. (1993). *Japan's Capitalism: creative defeat and beyond*. Cambridge: Cambridge University Press.

Yoshikawa, H. (2002). *Japan's Lost Decade*. Tokyo: The International House of Japan. Translated by Charles H. Stewart from Japanese edition (1999), *Tenkanki no Nihon Keizai*. Tokyo: Iwanami Shoten.

Data Sources

Asterisk (*) after parentheses in data source section shows a survey year and the publication is the following year (one year later).

ACB on SSS (Advisory Council Bureau on Social Security System) of MCA (Management and Coordination Agency) (1959–1975). *Shakai Hosho Tokei Nenpo* [Annual Report on Social Security Statistics]. Tokyo: Shakai Hoken Hoki Kenkyu-kai.

CAO (Cabinet Office) (2007). *Kokumin Seikatsu Hakusho* [White Paper on National Living Life]. Tokyo: Jinji Gaho-sha.

Council of Economic Advisers (–2009). *Economic Report of the President*. Washington, DC: The United States Government Printing Office.

DNA (Department of National Accounts) of ERI (Economic Research Institute), EPA (Economic Planning Agency) (1998). 1996 Nen no Mushorodo no Kahei-hyoka [The value of Unpaid Work 1996]. www5.cao.go.jp/98/g/19981105 g-unpaid.html.

DNA (Department of National Accounts) of ESRI (Economic and Social Research Institute), CAO (a) (2001–2008). *Annual Report on National Accounts*. Tokyo: Media Land Co. Ltd.

DNA (Department of National Accounts) of ESRI (Economic and Social Research Institute), CAO (b) (2007). *Annual Report on Prefectural Accounts*. Tokyo: Media Land Co. Ltd.

EPA (Economic Planning Agency) of GoJ (Government of Japan) (a) (2000). *Annual Report on National Accounts*. Tokyo: Printing Bureau, Ministry of Finance.

ESRI (Economic and Social Research Institute), CAO (a) (–2009). *Kakei Shohi no Doko* [Consumer Behavior Survey]. Tokyo: National Printing Bureau.

ESRI (Economic and Social Research Institute), CAO (b) (2001–2004). *Keizai Yoran* [Statistics Handbook on Economy]. Tokyo: Printing Bureau, Ministry of Finance. (See IB of EPA for (–2000).)

FSA (Financial Services Agency), Japanese Government (2008). Yokin Toriatsukai Kikan no Jokyo-toh nitsuite [The State of Loans under the Risk Management in Deposit Taking Financial Institutions] (Homepage: www.fsa.go.jp/en/regulated/npl/20080215.html).

GIOMS (Government Information Office of Minister's Secretariat), CAO (2006). Public Opinion Survey on National Life. www8.cao.go.jp/survey/index.html.

IB of EPA (Investigation Bureau of the Economic Planning Agency) (a) (1963, 1984–2000). *Keizai Yoran* [Statistics Handbook on Economy]. Tokyo: Printing Bureau, Ministry of Finance.

IB of EPA (Investigation Bureau of the Economic Planning Agency) (b) (1963, 1970, 1977). *Shohi to Chochiku no Doko* [Trends of Consumption and Savings]. Tokyo: Printing Bureau, Ministry of Finance.

International Department of BoJ (Bank of Japan) (1996–2000). *Comparative Economic and Financial Statistics: Japan and Other Major Countries*. Tokyo: The Tokiwa Sogo Service Co., Ltd.

Iwanami Shoten (ed.) (2001). *Kindai Nihon Sogo Nenpyo* [Comprehensive Chronological Table of Modern Japan], 4th ed. Tokyo: Iwanami Shoten.

Japan Real Estate Institute (2009). (Home page) www.reinet.or.jp/documentation/index.html#011.

Japan Statistical Association (2006). *Historical Statistics of Japan, New Edition*, Vol. 1–5. Tokyo: Japan Statistical Association.

MHLW (Ministry of Health, Labour and Welfare) (2004, 2006, 2008). *Kosei Rodo Hakusho* [Annual Survey of Health, Welfare and Labour]. Tokyo: Gyosei. (www.mhlw.go.jp/wp/hakusyo/index.html)

NI of PSSR (National Institute of Population and Social Security Research) (2009). "Seikatsu Hogo" ni Kansuru Koteki Tokei Data Ichiran [Official Statistical Data of "Livelihood Protection"] (www.ipss.go.jp/s-info/j/seiho/seihoH21.xls)

PRI (Policy Research Institute) of MoF (Ministry of Finance) (–2009). *Hojin Kigyo Tokei Nenpo* [Financial Statistics of Corporations]. Data are obtained from (www:mof.go.jp/1c002.htm).

QLPB (Quality-of-Life Policy Bureau) of EPA (1992). *Yutakasa Shihyo to Kongo no Kokumin Seikatsu: Shinpojumu Shiryo* [A Quality-of-Life Index and National Life in the Future: Resources for Symposium]. Tokyo: Quality-of-Life Policy Bureau, Economic Planning Agency.

RSD (Research and Statistics Department) of BoJ (Bank of Japan) (a) (1985, 1986, 1993, 1996)*. *Economic Statistics Annual*. Tokyo: The Credit Information Company of Japan, Ltd.

RSD (Research and Statistics Department) of BoJ (Bank of Japan) (b) (2009). *Bank of Japan Statistics*. Tokyo: Sun Partners Co., Ltd.

RSD (Research and Statistics Department) of BoJ (Bank of Japan) (c) (1977–1991). *Comparative Economic and Financial Statistics: Japan and Other Major Countries*. Tokyo: The Credit Information Company of Japan, Ltd.

SB of MCA (Statistics Bureau of Management and Coordination Agency) (a) (1987, 1991, 1993)*. *Annual Report on the Consumer Price Index*. Tokyo: Japan Statistical Association. (Note that from 2001, SB of MCA was named as SB of Ministry of Public Management, Home Affairs, Posts and Telecommunications, and in 2006, renamed as the SB of MIAC (Statistics Bureau, Ministry of International Affairs and Communications).

SB of MCA (Statistics Bureau of Management and Coordination Agency) (b) (–2001)*. *Annual Report on the Family Income and Expenditure Survey*. Tokyo: Japan Statistical Association.

SB of MCA (Statistics Bureau of Management and Coordination Agency) (c) (–2001)*. *Annual Report on the Labour Force Survey*. Tokyo: Japan Statistical Association.

SB of MCA (Statistics Bureau of Management and Coordination Agency) (d) (1988), *Comprehensive Time Series Report on the Family Income and Expenditure Survey 1947–1986*. Tokyo: Japan Statistical Association.

SB of MCA (Statistics Bureau of Management and Coordination Agency) (e) (–2001)*. *Family Savings Survey*. Tokyo: Japan Statistical Association.

SB of MCA (Statistics Bureau of Management and Coordination Agency) (f) (1977–2001). *Social Indicators by Prefecture*. Tokyo: Japan Statistical Association.

SB of MIAC (Statistics Bureau, Ministry of International Affairs and Communications) (a) (–2007)*. *Annual Report on the Consumer Price Index*. Tokyo: Japan Statistical Association.

SB of MIAC (Statistics Bureau, Ministry of International Affairs and Communications) (b) (–2007)*. *Annual Report on the Family Income and Expenditure Survey <Income and Expenditure>*. Tokyo: Japan Statistical Association.

SB of MIAC (Statistics Bureau, Ministry of International Affairs and Communications) (c) (–2007)*. *Annual Report on the Family Income and Expenditure Survey <Savings and Liabilities>*. Tokyo: Japan Statistical Association.

SB of MIAC (Statistics Bureau, Ministry of International Affairs and Communications) (d) (–2007)*. *Annual Report on the Labour Force Survey*. Tokyo: Japan Statistical Association.

SB of MIAC (Statistics Bureau, Ministry of International Affairs and Communications) (e) (–2007)*. *National Survey of Family Income and Expenditure*. Tokyo: Japan Statistical Association.

SB of MIAC (Statistics Bureau, Ministry of International Affairs and Communications) (f) (2008). *Population by Labour Force Status, Industry and Occupation* (2005 Population Census of Japan, Overview Series No. 6). Tokyo: Japan Statistical Association

SB of MIAC (Statistics Bureau, Ministry of International Affairs and Communications) (g) (–2007). *Social Indicators by Prefecture*. Tokyo: Japan Statistical Association.

SB of MIAC (Statistics Bureau, Ministry of International Affairs and Communications) (h) (2009). *2005 Population Census of Japan*, Vol. 5, No. 1. Tokyo: Japan Statistical Association.

SID (Statistics and Information Department), Minister's Secretariat, MHLW (–2008). *Kokumin Seikatsu Kiso Chosa* [Comprehensive Survey of Living Condition of the People on Health and Welfare]. Tokyo: Kosei Tokei Kyokai.

Study Group on Activation Policy for the Depopulated Areas (Kaso Chiiki Kasseika Taisaku Kenkyukai, cooperated) (1999). *Kaso Taisaku no Genkyo* [The Present Situation of Countermeasures towards the Depopulated Areas]. Tokyo: Tokyo Kansho Fukyu Co. Ltd.

Survey Section of PDMS (Policy Department of Minister's Secretariat), MHLW (–2005 survey). *Shotoku Saibunpai Chosa Hokokusho* [Report on the Survey of Income Redistribution]. Tokyo: Kosei Rodosho Daijinkanbo Seisaku Chosashitsu. wwwdbtk.mhlw.go.jp/toukei/kohyo/indexkk_6_4.html.

Tokyo Stock Exchange (2008). *Monthly Statistics Report*, No. 617 (March).

Watanabe, T., Skrzypczak, E.R., and Snowdon, P. (eds.) (2003). *Kenkyusha's Japanese-English Dictionary*, 5th ed. Tokyo: Kenkyusha.

Index

Breinigsville, PA USA
20 August 2010
243810BV00003B/16/P